THE 7-FIGURE MACHINE

YOUR ULTIMATE ROADMAP TO
ENDLESS EARNINGS
AND **FINANCIAL FREEDOM**

DR. NOAH ST. JOHN

MEDIA

MEDIA

Published 2024 by Gildan Media LLC
aka G&D Media
www.GandDmedia.com

AFFORMATIONS®, iAfform® Audios, Making Success Automatic®, Permission to Succeed®, and Power Habits® are registered trademarks of Noah St. John and Success Clinic International, LLC.

Any mention of earnings or income should not be construed as representative of fixed or standard earnings. This book is not intended to provide personalized legal, accounting, financial, or investment advice. Readers are encouraged to seek the counsel of competent professionals with regard to such matters. The Author and Publisher specifically disclaim any liability, loss, or risk that is incurred as a consequence, directly or indirectly, of the use and application of any of the contents of this work.

The author of this book does not dispense medical advice or prescribe the use of any technique as a form of treatment for physical, emotional, or medical problems without the advice of a physician, either directly or indirectly. The intent of the author is to offer information of a general nature to help you in your quest for emotional and spiritual well-being. In the event you use any of the information in this book for yourself, which is your constitutional right, the author and the publisher assume no responsibility for your actions.

FIRST EDITION: 2024

Front cover design by Tom McKeveny

Library of Congress Cataloging-in-Publication Data is available upon request

ISBN: 978-1-7225-0677-3

10 9 8 7 6 5 4 3 2 1

PRAISE FOR NOAH ST. JOHN

"To say that Noah St. John changed our lives is the understatement of the century. Before hiring Noah as my personal coach, I had a brochure website that wasn't bringing in any money. Today, I have my own online store that makes me money in my sleep. Thank you, Noah, for bringing out the greatness in me that I didn't even know I had!"

—Dr. Stacey Cooper, Chiropractor

"Before I heard Noah speak, I had been a failure at everything I touched. After using his methods, I built the largest infill development company in Nashville with over $40 million in sales. Thank you, Noah; keep doing what you're doing because a lot of people need you!"

—Britnie Turner Keane,
CEO of Aerial Development Group

"I highly recommend Dr. Noah St. John as a keynote speaker because he's not only different from other speakers, he also truly cares about his clients and resonates on a deep emotional level with his audience. He's dynamic, impactful, inspiring, motivating, and professional—in short, the PERFECT speaker!"

—Lauren Ashley Kay, Meeting Planner

"Dr. Noah St. John has been a legend in the industry of speaking and motivating for many years. His reputation as a home run speaker, powerful coach, and performance expert is among the best in the world. More importantly, his home life, family, and ability to balance both business and the living of a wonderful life are inspiring to his peers and clients. He is an example to all who know him."

—Jason Hewlett, CSP, CPAE,
Author of *The Promise to the One*

"Noah's methods helped me get through a particularly challenging time in my life. If you're thinking about hiring Noah as a coach, trainer, or speaker, don't think about it another minute—just DO it, because his strategies have the power to change lives!"

—Mari Smith, Facebook Marketing Expert

"Noah's methods can transform your life and help you create the masterpiece you truly want and are capable of achieving."   —John Assaraf, Motivational Speaker
featured in *The Secret*

"Noah's training was instrumental in helping me bounce back and into major profits. His insights on removing head trash are unlike anything I've ever seen!"

—Ray Higdon, Author of *Time, Money, Freedom*

"Noah St. John helped me gain the mental edge I was looking for. His methods helped me perform at my highest level without strain, and I saw better results immediately using his system."

—Andre Branch, NFL Football Player

"Before being coached by Noah, I was holding myself back out of fear. Since working with Noah, I've built a multimillion-dollar company in less than two years. I highly recommend coaching with Noah, because I guarantee it will change your life, like it changed mine!"

—Tim Taylor, Real Estate Professional

"Noah St. John has been at the forefront of the business coaching industry for more than two decades now. He's the best in the business when it comes to helping entrepreneurs skyrocket their results in record time. If you want to take your business to a whole new level without the stress or overwhelm, hire Noah St. John TODAY. You'll be glad you did!"

—Anik Singal, CEO

ALSO BY NOAH ST. JOHN, PhD

The 7-Figure Expert: Your Ultimate Guide to a Life of More Impact, Influence, and Financial Freedom

The 7-Figure Chiropractor: Your Ultimate Guide to Scale Up Your Practice and Live a Freedom Lifestyle

The 7-Figure Life: How to Leverage The 4 Focus Factors for More Wealth and Happiness

Power Habits®: The New Science for Making Success Automatic®

The Power Habits® of Unstoppable Self-Confidence

AFFORMATIONS®: The Miracle of Positive Self-Talk

Millionaire AFFORMATIONS®: The Magic Formula That Will Make You Rich

Millionaire AFFORMATIONS® Journal: The Magic Habit Formula That Will Make You Rich

Get Rid of Your Head Trash about Money

The Secret Code of Success

Permission to Succeed®

Available at NoahStJohn.com
or wherever books are sold

This book is dedicated to #Afformers and
#AfformationWarriors around the world:
Those brave souls who ask better questions
to make this a better world
for all of God's creatures.

And to my beautiful wife, Babette,
for being the best example of a Loving Mirror
I've ever met.

Contents

How This Book Was Written—and Why

*A great book is the lifeblood of a
master spirit, embalmed and treasured
up on purpose to a life beyond life.*
—STEPHEN COVEY

When I launched my global coaching and online training company, SuccessClinic.com, in October 1997, I was living in a 300-square-foot basement apartment in Hadley, Massachusetts. I had $800 in my bank account and a book on html. I also had . . .

- No marketing experience
- No sales knowledge
- No business acumen
- No email list
- No clue how to run a successful online business

Keep in mind that this was in the late nineties, when the world was still on dial-up; there was no Facebook, YouTube, Instagram, or TikTok; in fact, Google hadn't even launched yet (it's true: my company is actually seven months older than Google!). In short, there were none of the modern tools and conveniences that we take for granted today.

Yet I did have one thing going for me—a deep, burning desire to, as Steve Jobs put it, "put a dent in the universe." Meaning that I truly wanted to make a difference, to help people, to have a lasting *impact* on the world. I was determined to uncover exactly how to do that.

Here's what happened next . . .

I self-published my first book, *Permission to Succeed*®, by going to the local copy shop and printing 100 tape-bound copies. (Yes, it was actually bound with a piece of tape, because that's the cheapest way they could publish my book.)

Then I drove around to local bookstores (this was when bookstores were a thing) and asked them if they'd like to take my book on consignment. Most said no; a few said yes.

So I began giving talks at bookstores and selling a few copies of my self-published book.

Then, as luck would have it, I got to meet Jack Canfield, coauthor of the Chicken Soup for the Soul book series, at a ceremony where he was being given a lifetime achievement award. I handed him a copy of my self-published book and asked if he might be interested in it.

I was hoping he might send it to his agent; instead, he offered to send it directly to his publisher. Eight weeks later, that publisher called me and offered me my first publishing deal.

Naturally, I was ecstatic. This was the big break I'd been hoping for!

When *Permission to Succeed* was published by the Chicken Soup for the Soul publisher in 1999, I figured this was how it would work:

Week one, my book would be published.

Week two, I'd be on *The Oprah Winfrey Show*.

Week three, I'd be a millionaire.

Needless to say, it didn't work out that way.

In fact, when my book came out, I was shocked at how little my publisher did to market it. I honestly expected that being published by a house of that stature meant that they were going to do all (or at least, the majority) of the marketing for me.

Not so much.

In fact, the way the publishing world works is, you (the author) do all of the work, and the publisher keeps most of the money.

Why would anyone agree to this?

Because of the one thing that you, the author, don't have the resources to do: distribution. Meaning that the publisher can (or should) get you into all the bookstores and other sales outlets that are simply too expensive or time-consuming for the average author to get in.

It was my first lesson in disappointment—the first of many.

Around this time, I slowly began to realize that as an author of one book, I had a big problem: I was the author of one book. If I wanted to make serious money in this industry, I either had to sell a heck of a lot of that one book or come up with other ways to bring in money.

So I began going to different seminars and taking trainings from the big marketing gurus in order to learn how to bring in money from my expertise. There were many of them—over ninety-three at last count (and I've got the spreadsheet to prove it).

THE MARKETING GURUS SUCK AT TEACHING.

There was just one problem: the marketing gurus suck at teaching.

The painful and expensive lesson I learned is, the marketing gurus are great at self-marketing and self-promotion, but they can't teach or coach their way out of a paper bag.

Have you ever experienced something like this? You pay a marketing guru all this money and devote your time ... only to discover that there's no there, there.

Meaning, what they actually *do* and what they *tell* you to do are vastly different things. They're doing something over here, while telling you to do this other thing over there.

That always seemed wrong to me. Yet I could never find anyone who could actually help me with what I wanted to do—get my message out to the world in a much bigger way.

Eventually, I realized that I was going to have to figure all this out on my own, which, let's face it, is a lousy way to learn. Because the one thing we can never get back is time.

In fact, the biggest problem with trial and error is that last part—error! Nevertheless, after so many disappointments, broken promises, and paying so many ... how can I put this nicely? ... lying sociopaths, I realized that if it was going to be, it was up to me.

So I became more determined than ever to figure it out. And since making that decision, I assembled the 7-Figure Machine Framework, which I'm sharing with you in this book.

Now this may be the first marketing book you've read, or it might be the hundredth. Either way, I'm willing to bet that you've experienced or are currently experiencing one or more of the following challenges in your business:

1. Difficulty attracting consistent, quality leads.
2. Struggle with converting leads into paying customers.
3. Challenges in scaling up business operations efficiently.
4. Inadequate cash flow management.
5. Overwhelm from wearing multiple hats.
6. Maintaining a competitive edge in the market.
7. Navigating digital marketing complexities.
8. Finding and retaining skilled employees.
9. Time management and productivity issues.
10. Balancing work and personal life.
11. Managing customer expectations and satisfaction.
12. Keeping up with technological advancements.
13. Successfully developing and launching new products or services.
14. Understanding and utilizing social media effectively.
15. Managing stress and burnout.
16. Creating a loyal customer base.
17. Ensuring consistent quality of products or services.
18. Overcoming fear of failure and risk-taking.

19. Coping with competition and market saturation.
20. Developing effective communication strategies.
21. Crafting a compelling business story.
22. Aligning business goals with personal values.
23. Staying motivated and focused on long-term goals.
24. Seeing your competitors who aren't as good as you get more money, attention, and recognition than you do.

All of the entrepreneurs and business owners that I've coached over the last twenty-five years have faced one or more of these challenges, which is why I'll address them in this book and give you specific strategies to overcome them.

CAN YOU RELATE TO ANY OF THESE?

Whom This Book Is For

This book is for you if you're a business owner or entrepreneur who . . .

- Wants to scale your business but feels overwhelmed by the process.
- Faces cash flow issues that hinder business growth.

- Feels drained from juggling multiple roles in your business.
- Needs to maintain a competitive edge, but isn't sure how.
- Is confused by the complexities of digital marketing strategies.
- Wants to hire and retain the right team but struggles with the process.
- Seeks to improve time management and productivity.
- Aims for a better work-life balance while running a successful business.

These are the common challenges and aspirations of the business owners and entrepreneurs I'm privileged to coach and mentor every day, which means this book can be highly relevant and valuable to you.

Which is why I now want to give you the top 8 ways to get the most from this book.

The Top 8 Ways to Get the Most from This Book

Knowledge isn't power until it is applied.

—DALE CARNEGIE

1. Know What You Want and Why You Want It

Setting a clear goal is the first and most critical step in leveraging the full potential of this book. It involves defining what success looks like for your business and determining the specific outcomes you wish to achieve.

This clarity of purpose transforms the reading experience from passive consumption to active engagement, enabling you to focus on the parts of the book that are most relevant to your objectives.

By aligning this book's teachings with these well-defined objectives, you can create a roadmap that guides your business decisions and strategies.

2. Take Good Notes

Taking notes as you read this book is more than just a way to remember content: it's a strategy to engage deeply with the ideas presented. As you read, jot down insights, questions, and revelations. These notes will become a valuable resource that you can turn to as you apply the book's teachings to your business.

Also, your notes can serve as a catalyst for action. They're not just a record of what you've read; they're a blueprint for implementation. By regularly reviewing your notes, you can identify actionable steps, track your progress, and see where you need to make adjustments. This habit turns static learning into dynamic growth.

Moreover, the act of taking notes fosters a deeper connection with the material. It's an active form of learning that encourages you to think critically and creatively. Your notes are a dialogue with the book—a way to test your understanding and push beyond the page.

3. Reflect on Your Current Challenges

Reflecting on your business challenges while reading this book is crucial for tailored growth and development. As you encounter various concepts and strategies, consider how they apply to the specific obstacles you're facing. This reflection will transform theory into practice, making the content directly relevant and immediately applicable to your unique situation.

REFLECT ON YOUR CHALLENGES, AND DECIDE WHAT YOU WANT TO FOCUS ON FIRST.

In fact, each chapter in this book provides insights that might resonate differently depending on your current business challenges. Whether you're facing issues with lead generation, client retention, or scaling your business, use these moments to pause and think about how you can apply the lessons learned to these areas.

The true value of this book lies in its application to real-world problems. By continuously relating the content back to your specific business challenges, you create a personalized action plan.

4. Seek Clarity

As you progress through each chapter, if any concept or strategy isn't immediately clear, take the time to reread and contemplate it. This commitment to understanding ensures that you fully grasp the ideas and their potential impact on your business.

In your pursuit of clarity, don't hesitate to look for additional resources or examples that can shed more light on these topics. Sometimes a different perspective or a real-world case study can make a challenging concept more accessible.

As your business evolves, so will your understanding of these concepts. Revisiting chapters with a fresh perspective can reveal new insights and deepen your comprehension, ensuring you're always aligned with the best practices for your business growth.

5. Do the Exercises

If you don't do the exercises in this book, it won't make any difference in your life or business, will it? These exercises are designed to challenge your current thinking, expand your perspectives, and catalyze growth in your business strategy and operations.

This hands-on experience is invaluable, as it not only reinforces your learning, but also boosts your confidence in applying these strategies in real-world scenarios.

These exercises are not just tasks to be completed; they are stepping stones to deeper understanding and more effective business practices to create the life and business of your dreams.

6. Join the Discussion

To join an active community of like-minded individuals, I invite you to participate in our Facebook group, The 7-Figure Life. It's a platform where dynamic discussions unfold, enriching your learning experience. Connect with us at Facebook.com/groups/7FigureLife.

By participating, you'll gain access to diverse perspectives and insights that can enhance your understanding. It's a chance to engage with fellow readers, share experiences, and discuss the application of book strategies in various business scenarios.

7. Get Help

Getting help while working through the concepts of this book will significantly enhance your learning experience; it will also enable you to reach your goals faster, easier, and with far less stress.

Recognizing when you need external guidance or support is a strength, not a weakness. It's an opportunity to gain deeper insights, troubleshoot specific challenges, and accelerate your progress. An external perspective can provide clarity, accountability, and expert advice tailored to your unique business situation.

Seeking professional guidance can also help you navigate complex strategies or implement changes more effectively. Working with a coach or consultant can provide the necessary structure and motivation to move forward with confidence, ensuring that you're not just understanding the concepts but are also effectively applying them to your business.

SEEKING HELP IS A STRENGTH, NOT A WEAKNESS.

For personalized assistance and a customized, tailored approach to your business challenges, I encourage you to schedule a complimentary Breakthrough Consultation, because this session is your golden opportunity to discuss your specific needs and how you can apply the principles of this book to achieve your business goals faster, easier and with far less stress.

Visit **BreakthroughwithNoah.com** to book your complimentary Breakthrough Consultation and take a significant step towards your business success.

8. Remember This: Money Loves Speed

In the world of business and entrepreneurship, there's a principle that often goes understated yet holds immense power: the fact that *money loves speed*.

This isn't just a catchphrase: it embodies a fundamental truth about how momentum and quick action can significantly influence your financial success. The faster you can move from concept to execution, the faster you can test ideas, refine strategies, and find what works for you.

Speed builds momentum, and momentum is a powerful ally. When you act quickly, you create a series of events that build upon each other, generating energy and forward motion.

Ideas alone don't generate income; action does. Speed in execution transforms your ideas into tangible products or services, creating real value for your customers. It's this value that translates into income. By acting swiftly, you turn potential into profit.

As you build your 7-Figure Machine, keep this principle in mind. Let speed be your ally, and watch as it helps you navigate the path to financial success with greater agility and confidence!

Introduction

How Your Life Can Change In Just 12 Weeks

Believe you can, and you're halfway there.
—THEODORE ROOSEVELT

In November 2020, the world was in the depths of the global pandemic. For months, it seemed as though everything was shut down and our future was uncertain. It was all fear, fear, fear.

On the Saturday before Thanksgiving that year, I woke up at five in the morning with a vision. It came completely out of the blue, and it said, *We're supposed to move.*

Have you ever had one of those inner knowings that told you something that didn't make any logical sense—yet you listened to it, because you knew it came from your higher knowing or intuitive self? You've had that happen to you too, right?

When this happened to me, my response was, *What do you mean, we're supposed to move?*

My wife, Babette, and I were living in a nice, upper-middle-class home in a nice neighborhood, so moving to a new house was the furthest thing from my mind.

Yet I couldn't shake the inner knowing that woke me up early that morning. So I thought, *Maybe we can move in, say, six months to a year. After all, there's no hurry, right?*

So I got out of bed, turned on my computer, and started looking on real estate websites for homes in my area. Click, click, click—with no sense of urgency or even knowing what I was looking for.

Suddenly, I came upon a house—no, a mansion—no, a mansion on a hill—no, a mansion on a hill in a beautiful location—and I thought, *What?*

This house is *stunning.*

This house is *incredible.*

This house is a *mansion on a hill.*

It's *in my price range.*

It's *10 minutes from where I'm sitting right now.*

And *the price just dropped,*

And *there was going to be an open house the next day*—yes, the Sunday before Thanksgiving, 2020.

So I woke up Babette and said, "Honey, wanna go look at a house tomorrow?"

She said, "Sure!"

The next day, as we pulled up the driveway to this magnificent mansion, she took one look at the house, and said, "I'm packing tonight."

Eighty-three days later, we moved into that magnificent mansion on a hill. Yes, that's just one day less than 12 weeks!

In fact, we even celebrated our tenth wedding anniversary in our new mansion on a hill. So it's true:

your life can change in just 12 short weeks—if you're willing to take the *action* to make it happen!

Plus, as an added bonus, I was able to pay off our mortgage 27 years early as a result of following the very principles I'll teach you in this book.

What does this story mean for you?

I PAID OFF MY MORTGAGE 27 YEARS EARLY BY FOLLOWING THE PRINCIPLES IN THIS BOOK.

Whether this is the first business growth book you've ever read or the hundredth, one thing I know about you (because you're reading this right now) is that you're passionate about wanting to improve your life.

I'm Just like You

Like you, I'm passionate about self-improvement. You see, I grew up poor in a rich neighborhood. I know that's a total cliché, but it's true. I grew up in a little town called Kennebunkport, Maine—which happens to be one of the wealthiest communities in New England.

However, my family was dirt-poor. I mean that literally, because we lived at the bottom of a dirt road in a drafty, unfinished house that my parents ended up losing to foreclosure when I was just fifteen years old.

What I remember most about my childhood is my parents arguing all the time. What did they argue about? You're right—money . . . and the fact that we didn't have any.

Like millions of other parents, they worked hard and sacrificed to put food on the table and keep our family fed. But no matter how hard they tried, they could never seem to get ahead.

That's why, growing up, I saw firsthand the enormous chasm between the haves—which was everyone else in the community—and the have-nots, which was my family.

That's also why, from a very young age, I was determined that I was not going to live a life of poverty, fear, lack and not-enoughness—even though that was the only life I had ever known.

The problem was that I didn't have anyone I could turn to, who could help me, coach me, or teach me how to be successful.

GROWING UP, I EXPERIENCED FIRSTHAND THE GAP BETWEEN THE HAVES AND HAVE-NOTS.

So I turned to the only resource I had—the town library. Growing up, I would spend all of my days after school in the library, reading books on personal and spiritual growth—the classics by authors like Dale Carnegie, Napoleon Hill, Stephen Covey, Wayne Dyer, and more.

Many years later, when I was a religious studies major in college, I would drive around in my 1986 Subaru station wagon listening to self-improvement audiotapes (yes, this was when audiotapes were still a thing!).

My Dream to Make a Difference

Year after year, I would daydream and think to myself, "Wouldn't it be amazing if I could be a best-selling author, keynote speaker, and in-demand coach? Wouldn't it be incredible if people were driving around in their cars listening to *my* audio programs?"

In 1997, I had two epiphanies that changed the course of my life, when I discovered the essential missing piece in the field of mental health and personal development. That led me to write and self-publish my first book, *Permission to Succeed*.

WHEN MY CLIENTS FOLLOW MY SYSTEM, THEY GET LIFE-CHANGING RESULTS.

Then I published another book, and another, and yet another . . .

After I'd been in business for over ten years, I had written nine books, authored hundreds of articles, coached 7- and 8-figure CEOs, and consulted with leading companies and organizations on personal growth and business development. And I kept seeing the difference that my work was making in the lives of my coaching clients, like . . .

- Mike C. from New York doubled his income *twice* in 12 weeks.
- Susan S. from California went from $60,000 in debt to a six-figure income in less than 12 weeks.
- Thomesa L. from Arizona *tripled* her investment in the first two weeks
- Charles P. from North Carolina added an additional $1.8 million in ten months.
- Steven's business increased by 800 percent in less than 12 weeks.
- Adam's company went from being stuck at $4 million to over $20 million in revenues in less than 18 months.
- . . . and hundreds more.

Over and over again, I saw firsthand that when my clients followed my formula, they kept getting amazing results.

That's how, years after I was driving around in my raggedy Subaru station wagon, dreaming of the day I would be a best-selling author, keynote speaker, and in-demand mental health coach, my dream finally came true.

Welcome to Your New Life

The true story I just shared with you is only one example of what can happen when you start to apply the framework that I'll be sharing with you in this book.

The point of this story is that, for years, I *wished* that someday my dream would come true. I fervently *hoped* it would happen. Yet *wishing* and *hoping* do *not* make things happen! It wasn't until I applied the strategies I'll teach you in this book that I finally developed the confidence to take action in the face of my fears.

What does this mean for you? When you apply the framework I'll teach you in this book, you too can create multiple streams of income—which will enable you to do things you never thought were possible for you!

I'll also be sharing real-life stories of some of my coaching clients who implemented my 7-Figure Machine Formula and saw incredible transformations in their lives and businesses.

Finally, remember these words:

Napoleon Hill, author of *Think and Grow Rich*, said: "Those who reach decisions promptly and definitely know what they want and generally get it. The leaders in every walk of life decide quickly and firmly."

W. Clement Stone, insurance magnate and inspirational speaker, said: "The greatest enemy of wealth isn't a mindset issue. It isn't access to resources. It isn't upbringing or circumstances. The greatest enemy of wealth is delay."

Dr. Noah says: "Procrastination is the assassination of your destination."

Don't let the ghosts of fear, perfectionism, and procrastination keep you from having the income, impact, and influence you desire. Take inspired action in the face of fear—and I'll be here to help you, every step of the way.

Welcome to your new life!

Remember: I believe in you.

Your Coach,

Noah St. John, PhD

*Creator of The 7-Figure Machine
and The 12-Week Breakthrough*

1

My 7-Figure Offer Secrets

*Every successful business starts
with one successful offer.*
—NOAH ST. JOHN

I n the world of business, your offer is the heartbeat of your success. It's not simply what you sell; it's the solution you provide, the problem you solve, and the transformation you promise. Whether you're just starting out or you've been in business for years, the essence of a successful offer remains the same.

The core of a magnetic offer lies in its ability to resonate with your clients. It's not just about what you think is valuable; it's about understanding and meeting the deep-seated needs and desires of those you serve. So, as we progress, keep in mind that a magnetic offer is one that aligns perfectly with the aspirations of your clients while staying true to your vision and values.

Understanding and Meeting Market Needs

Successful offers stem from a deep understanding of market needs. As we dive deeper into my 7-Figure Machine Framework, it's crucial to align your offer with the real, often unspoken desires of your target audience. This section will guide you through identifying those needs and structuring your offers accordingly.

Where do we start? We start by dissecting market problems. Whether it's a need for better health, increased wealth, or fulfilling relationships, your offer should address core human desires. For instance, if you're in the health sector, your offer might focus not just on weight loss, but on the transformative journey towards a healthier, more energetic life.

When it comes to magnetic offers, specificity is key. Your offer shouldn't just hover over a broad topic: it needs to pinpoint a specific problem and present a clear, compelling solution.

Let's take my journey as an example. Over twenty-five years ago, I realized the need for a proven system that helps people achieve success without the constant struggle. This realization led to the creation of specific solutions that solve this core problem.

The Three Types of Magnetic Offers

The beauty of this framework lies in its flexibility. Going back to my example, I help people stop stopping themselves from the level of success they're capable of. That's the essence of what I do and have been doing for over a quarter century.

How do I deliver that solution? When I started out, I only had one offer: a book. As we all know, a book sells for about twenty bucks—which means you have to sell a heck of a lot of books in order to make enough money to live on, let alone have a six- or seven-figure business.

I realized that I'd better create additional offers that would still deliver the same outcome for my customers and clients but had an even greater value than a book.

While a book can be an excellent starting point to help your customers get a result, many people are looking for more—more time, more attention, more hand-holding, more accountability.

That's when I realized there are three types of magnetic offers:

1. Done for You
2. Done with You
3. Do It Yourself

Done for You Offers

With Done for You offers, the service provider (that is, you) handles all aspects of the task or project, delivering a complete, ready-to-use solution for the client. For a business owner, Done for You offers have the following pros and cons:

Pros

1. **Higher revenue potential.** You can command higher prices because of the comprehensive nature of the service.
2. **Client satisfaction.** High-quality, complete solutions can lead to greater client satisfaction and loyalty.
3. **Niche expertise.** Allows businesses to specialize and develop deep expertise in specific areas.
4. **Market differentiation.** Full-service offerings can set a business apart from competitors who offer more fragmented services.

Cons

1. **Resource-intensive.** Requires more time, effort, and possibly more staff to deliver the service.
2. **Scalability challenges.** More challenging to scale because of the intensive nature of the service.
3. **Client dependence.** Risk of overreliance on a few high-value clients for significant revenue.
4. **Complexity in management.** Managing complex projects can require sophisticated systems and processes.

Seven Examples of Done for You Offers

1. **Managed SEO services.** Complete handling of a company's SEO (search engine optimization) efforts.
2. **Social media account management.** Running and managing all aspects of social media accounts.
3. **Custom software development.** Tailor-made software solutions crafted for specific business needs.
4. **Full-service marketing campaigns.** Entire marketing campaigns, from strategy to execution.

5. **Personalized financial planning services.** comprehensive financial planning and management.

6. **Professional event planning.** Organizing and executing events, from logistics to execution.

7. **Complete website design and launch.** Building, designing, and launching a website.

The attraction of Done for You offers is clear from the perspectives of both client and business owner. However, keep in mind that there are certain things that simply don't lend themselves to a Done for You offer.

For example, imagine that you're a potential client who wants to get your body in great shape and have six-pack abs. You've heard that I'm the best personal trainer out there, because I coach Hollywood celebrities, professional athletes, and busy corporate executives.

You contact me through my website, and we have a personal consultation. I say to you, "OK, I'm 100 percent confident that I can help you get in amazing shape and reach your health and fitness goals. When I coach you, I'm going to give you an easy-to-follow, step-by-step meal plan, along with a proven exercise plan, as well as the support you need to get in the best shape of your life."

You say, "That sounds great, Noah. There's just one more thing."

"What's that?"

"I just want you to do my sit-ups so I get six-pack abs."

The fact is, there simply isn't a way to outsource certain things that individuals must do for themselves— for instance, exercise and personal growth. That's why there are certain things that you, as a business owner, simply won't be able to create Done for You offers for. However, that brings us to . . .

WOULDN'T IT BE GREAT IF WE COULD OUTSOURCE OUR SIT-UPS?

Done with You Offers

Done with You offers involve a collaborative approach whereby the service provider (for example, you) works alongside the client to achieve the desired outcome. This partnership model combines the expertise of the service provider with the client's direct involvement.

Here are some pros and cons of Done with You offers:

Pros

1. **Balanced workload.** Shared responsibilities can reduce the strain on your resources.
2. **Client engagement.** Fosters deeper client relationships and loyalty.
3. **Flexibility.** Easier to adapt and tailor services to individual client needs.
4. **Broader appeal.** Attracts clients who wish to be more hands-on.

Cons

1. **Time management.** Requires careful scheduling to balance client collaboration with other tasks.
2. **Client variability.** Success depends on the client's commitment and capabilities.
3. **Training needs.** Might require educating clients to ensure effective collaboration.
4. **Potentially lower revenue.** May not command as high a price as Done for You services.

Seven Examples of Done with You Offers

1. **Coaching sessions.** Personalized guidance while clients implement strategies.

2. **Marketing workshops.** Collaborative sessions for developing marketing strategies.

3. **Website development with client input.** Building a site with direct client involvement in design and content.

4. **Joint business strategy planning.** Working with clients to develop and refine their business strategies.

5. **Interactive financial advisory services.** Collaborative financial planning and management.

6. **Social media strategy sessions.** Developing and implementing social media strategies with client participation.

7. **Content creation collaboration.** Joint creation of content such as blogs, videos, or podcasts.

Done with You offers are my personal favorite, because they offer the benefits of commanding higher prices than Do It Yourself offers. I also get the joy and feeling of satisfaction of knowing that I have made a real difference in the lives of my clients.

Finally, we come to the third type of magnetic offer . . .

Do It Yourself Offers

Do It Yourself Offers are products or services designed for customers to independently use or implement, typically with guidance or a framework provided by you, the business owner, or service provider.

Pros

1. **Scalability.** Easier to scale, as these offers often require less direct time per client.
2. **Broader market reach.** Attracts a wider range of clients, including those who prefer self-guidance.
3. **Passive income potential.** Can provide ongoing income with less active involvement.
4. **Lower resource requirements.** Less intensive in terms of time and staffing.

Cons

1. **Limited pricing potential.** Usually priced lower than more personalized services.
2. **Less client interaction.** Reduced opportunities for building deep client relationships (however, Do It Yourself buyers can often become Done with You or Done for You buyers).

3. **Greater reliance on marketing.** Requires effective marketing for provider to reach a wider audience.

4. **Quality control.** The need to ensure that the self-service products maintain high standards.

Seven Examples of Do It Yourself Offers

1. **Online courses.** Self-paced learning on specific topics.

2. **Ebooks and guides.** Comprehensive instructions and insights in written form.

3. **Webinar series.** Prerecorded webinars covering various aspects of a subject.

4. **DIY (do-it-yourself) kits.** Packages with all necessary materials and instructions for a project.

5. **Software tools.** Applications or tools for business management or productivity.

6. **Subscription-based content libraries.** Access to a repository of resources and materials.

7. **Self-assessment tools.** Online tools for self-evaluation and strategic planning.

Of course, there are many more examples of Do It Yourself offers; this list merely scratches the surface.

Understanding and effectively implementing the three types of offers—Done for You, Done with You, and Do It Yourself—can significantly diversify and strengthen your business's service portfolio.

Each offer type caters to different client needs and preferences, allowing you to reach a broader audience. By balancing these offerings, you can maximize your company's revenue potential, enhance client satisfaction, and ensure a sustainable, scalable business model.

Now let's look at the next step of creating 7-Figure Offers.

Your X-Factor Method

Every day, as you scroll on social media, you are shown ads from a variety of advertisers. What is it that causes you to stop the scroll instead of continuing to scroll?

The answer lies partly in the way in which the information (offer) is presented. The human brain is very efficient: it is constantly trying to conserve energy. When you see something that makes your brain say, "Ah, I've seen that before" or "I know what this person's going to say," your

THIS IS WHY MOST ADVERTISING IS IGNORED.

brain will instinctively keep you scrolling (that is, ignoring the message).

The X-Factor Method

So how do you set yourself up so that your message and your offer are not ignored? One of the best places to start is by identifying what I call your *X-Factor Method*.

What does this mean? When we look at an offer, it really boils down to solving a human problem. Human problems can generally be categorized into four main types, each with its own set of subproblems:

Money Problems

- Debt and poor credit management.
- Inadequate savings or investments.
- Unstable income or job insecurity.
- Financial illiteracy or poor financial planning.
- Business financial challenges, like cash flow issues.

Health Problems

- Chronic diseases or acute illnesses.
- Mental health issues, including stress, anxiety, and depression.

- Poor nutrition and unhealthy lifestyles.
- Lack of access to healthcare or medical support.
- Age-related health concerns.

Relationship Problems

- Communication issues in personal or professional relationships.
- Struggles with finding or maintaining romantic relationships.
- Family conflicts, including parenting challenges.
- Social isolation or difficulty in making friends.
- Professional networking and collaboration issues.

Stress-Related Problems

- Work-related stress, including burnout.
- Stress from life changes, like moving or changing jobs.
- Emotional stress from personal issues or life events.
- Physical stress from lack of sleep or poor health.
- Financial stress.

Each of these categories encompasses a range of specific issues that individuals and companies commonly face, offering numerous opportunities for targeted solutions and support.

Identifying a market problem is about recognizing a specific need or challenge that your target audience faces. For instance, let's say you're in the wellness industry. You notice that many people struggle with sustainable weight loss. They lose weight only to regain it, leading to a cycle of frustration. This problem is not just about losing weight; it's about maintaining a healthy lifestyle.

Your expertise in nutrition and fitness can address this cycle, offering a solution that goes beyond temporary fixes to promote long-term health.

YOU NEED TO ADDRESS THE PROBLEM BEHIND THE PROBLEM.

Another example could be in digital marketing. For example, many small businesses struggle to make their mark online. They may have a website and social media presence but fail to generate meaningful engagement or sales. The problem isn't just the lack of online activity: it's a lack of targeted strategy that speaks directly to their ideal customers.

If your expertise lies in digital marketing, this is where you can step in, offering tailored strategies that help these businesses effectively reach and engage their audience.

In each case, the key is to dive deep into the specific challenges your target audience faces. It's not enough to identify a broad issue; you must understand the nuances and pain points that come with it.

This deep understanding allows you to create solutions that are not just effective but also highly sought after, because they address the real problems your clients face every day.

In summary, the first step of identifying your X-Factor Method requires keen observation, market research, and empathy for the challenges of your target audience. By aligning your solution with these challenges, you ensure your offer is relevant, impactful, and desirable to your target market.

Developing Your Magnetic Offer

Understanding what a magnetic offer truly is is crucial for creating compelling and effective products or services. A magnetic offer consists of 90 percent *outcome*—the transformation or change you promise to deliver to your clients—and 10 percent *service delivery*, which is how you deliver that transformation.

Your clients are more interested in the outcome or the destination they are being led to than in the specifics of the journey or the route they take to get there.

The crucial feature of this concept lies in its focus on the end result— the transformation. Your clients are seeking a change or solution to their problem, and your offer should clearly communicate the desired outcome. This perspective helps in crafting offers that are outcome-oriented, making them more appealing and effective.

However, many wannabe experts get this wrong by focusing too much on the service delivery—the features, process, or methodology they use—without adequately highlighting the outcome they provide. They mistakenly talk too much about the tools, techniques, and processes they use, while losing sight of the fact that the client simply desires the *result* that these tools and processes will bring them.

That's why I encourage my clients to do the following, to ensure they don't make this critical mistake . . .

Focus on the Destination, Not the Plane

What do I mean? Here's an example from real life.

When I take my family on a vacation to Hawaii, I'm completely focused on the goal: a safe, timely arrival at our desired destination. Naturally, we're going to reach our destination by flying on an airplane.

However, I don't care all that much about the features of the airplane we'll be on: for example, that it carries between 25,000 and 33,000 gallons of fuel; that it will be traveling at an average speed of 547 to 561 miles per hour; that the plane has between 240 to 340 seats; and so on.

No, all I really care about is the answer to this question: will this airplane deliver me and my family to our desired destination safely and on time?

In the world of business, your customers or clients are similarly goal-oriented. The fact is, they aren't overly concerned with the intricate details of your methods or tools—the "plane" in this analogy.

What truly matters to them is the destination, or the outcome they seek to achieve. This end result, the transformation or benefit they will receive, is the essence of your offer and what you should emphasize.

Misunderstanding this crucial point can lead to offers that, while rich in features and methodologies, fail to resonate with the client's core desires and needs. The key is to always bring the conversation back to the transformation or outcome that your client will experience. By doing so, you make your offer irresistible, because it directly addresses your client's ultimate goal.

Here's another example: when I started my career in the personal development industry in the 1990s, speakers would get onstage and make offers based on how much information they could stuff in their offer. They would say things like, "You get 37 DVDs, you get a 260-page workbook, you get 18 audios, etc., etc."

That was in the pre-Internet age. Nowadays, if you said something like that, your audience would say, "Are you kidding me?" because we are on information overload. Everyone has virtually unlimited access to an infinite amount of information.

As a result, your buyers don't care about information for information's sake anymore. Instead, you need to focus on the transformation that your product or service will give them and address the specific outcomes and improvements they are seeking. This shift reflects a deeper understanding of what truly adds value in an information-saturated world.

THIS IS HOW TO FOCUS ON THE DESTINATION, NOT THE PLANE.

Identify Your Unique Offer

Identifying your unique offer involves understanding the specific impact your product or service has on clients. Consider a client you've assisted and identify the concrete results they achieved. For example, a life coach might have helped a client increase their self-confidence, leading to a significant promotion at work.

The transformation here goes beyond just career advancement; it often extends to improved personal relationships and self-esteem. Therefore, reflect on what the client might have lost had they not worked with you. In this example, the client might have remained stuck in an unsatisfying job, affecting their overall happiness and potential earnings.

To identify your unique offer comprehensively, it's important to analyze in-depth case studies and map out your clients' transformational journey. Here's how to start:

1. **Case study analysis.** For instance, a financial advisor helps a client, Sarah, who is struggling with debt management and savings. After working together, Sarah clears her debt as well as establishing a robust savings plan.

2. **Specific results.** Sarah's specific result is not just debt clearance; she also gains financial literacy, enabling her to make informed financial decisions in the future.

3. **Broader transformation.** Beyond financial stability, Sarah experiences a reduction in stress and anxiety, leading to improved overall well-being and confidence in her financial future.

4. **Cost of inaction.** Had Sarah not sought help, she might have spiraled deeper into debt, faced severe financial constraints, and continued to endure high stress levels, affecting her mental health.

5. **Identifying pain points.** When identifying pain points for your ideal client, consider various aspects like financial insecurity, lack of savings, or poor investment choices. Highlight your expertise in areas like debt management, investment strategies, and financial planning.

6. **Tailoring your offer.** By understanding these specific challenges and transformations, tailor your offer to address not just the immediate problem (like debt) but also the underlying issues (like financial literacy), ensuring a comprehensive solution for your clients.

This detailed approach helps in formulating an offer that resonates deeply with potential clients, addressing their core issues and providing transformative results.

A Real-Life Example

Let me give you a real-life example of this concept in action. Whenever I bring on a new client, whether for one-on-one or group coaching, I always ask them one question: "How much do you think it's going to cost you over the next 12 months if you *don't* take out your head trash—the voice in your head that's keeping you stuck?"

I ask this question for two main reasons: (1) to get the prospect to think about something they've probably never thought about; and (2) to help the prospect understand the value of my offers.

For instance, I asked this question of one of my coaching prospects named Charles. He had been reading my books and scheduled a Breakthrough Consultation on our website.

On our very first call, I asked him, "Charles, how much do you think it's going to cost you over the next 12 months if you don't get this problem fixed, if we don't take out your head trash?"

Without batting an eye, he replied, "A million dollars. Noah, if I don't take out my head trash, I'm easily going to lose out on a million dollars in the next twelve months."

THIS ONE PROBLEM WAS COSTING MY CLIENT $1 MILLION A YEAR.

I said, "I hear this every day, and it's far more common than you might think. I tell you what—just give me 10 percent of that money, and

I'll find you $1 million in the next twelve months. In other words, if you gave me $1 and I gave you $10 in return, is that a good deal?"

He said, "Yes, that's a very good deal."

So he decided to hire me on the spot, and paid me 10 percent of $1 million ($100,000) to coach him one-on-one for twelve months. Guess what happened next . . .

As it turned out, I didn't find Charles $1 million in the next twelve months.

Instead, I found him $1.8 million in just 10 months!

Because of my coaching, I found him nearly $2 million that he would not have had if he hadn't followed my advice and taken out his head trash. Talk about hockey-stick growth!

Furthermore, because I helped him win his life back, Charles bought a new RV and went on a seven-week vacation with his wife. He told me that not only was he making more money than ever, he also had more *time* than ever. Now that's what we call a win-win-win!

This is the power of a unique offer in action: if Charles hadn't taken action, the pain of staying stuck and losing out on all that money would have been enormous. Because I made the offer irresistible, Charles was highly motivated to follow my instructions and remained open to my coaching.

Craft Your Unique Market Position

Creating a unique market position involves a deep understanding of the transformation you offer and effectively communicating it to resonate with your target audience. Here are seven steps to achieve this:

1. **Use impactful language.** Start by listing words and phrases that capture the essence of the transformation you provide. For example, if your specialty is enhancing productivity, words like "efficiency," "time-saving," and "life-changing" can be powerful.

2. **Highlight the negative.** If you're addressing pain points, turn up the pain. While this sounds counterintuitive, human beings will do more to avoid pain than to gain pleasure.

3. **Emotional resonance.** Choose words that evoke emotions. If you're a mental health coach, phrases like "peace of mind," "emotional freedom," and "renewed hope" can be impactful.

4. **Enter your buyer's mind.** Think about what your clients are likely pondering, and reflect that in your language. Phrases like "unlock your potential" or "achieve financial freedom" often enter their thought process.

5. **Craft a moniker.** Combine your method with your offer to create a unique title. For instance,

my monikers include "The Mental Health Coach to the Stars" and "The Father of Afformations®."

6. **Developing a slogan.** A catchy slogan or tagline that encapsulates your unique offer and method can significantly enhance your market position. For example, I created our slogan "Making Success Automatic®," which effectively conveys the essence of my products and services.

7. **Consistent messaging.** Ensure that your chosen words, phrases, moniker, and slogan are consistently used across all your marketing materials. This helps in building a strong, recognizable brand.

Three examples of people who've done this brilliantly are . . .

1. **Steve Jobs and Apple.** Jobs masterfully positioned Apple as a symbol of innovation and creativity. By focusing on sleek design and user experience, he differentiated Apple products in the tech market. His ability to blend technology with artistry created a unique brand identity that resonated emotionally with consumers.

2. **Gary Vaynerchuk.** Gary Vee's straightforward, no-nonsense approach to marketing and entrepreneurship has set him apart. He focuses on the "why it matters" of hustle and hard work,

combined with savvy social media use, offering a blend of inspiration and practical advice that appeals to a wide audience.

3. **Seth Godin.** Seth Godin stands out for his unique approach to marketing and branding. Known for his concept of "permission marketing," Godin advocates for creating products and content so good that they earn the audience's attention rather than interrupting it. His ability to simplify complex marketing principles into relatable and memorable concepts, coupled with his prolific writing and speaking, has established him as a trusted and distinct voice in the marketing world.

Your unique market position is a blend of what you offer and how you communicate it. It's about making your service stand out in a crowded market by highlighting its unique benefits and emotional impact to your ideal buyers.

Which brings us to the final step of creating 7-Figure Offers . . .

Determine Your Ideal Target Market

Determining your target market is crucial for the success of your business. To create a more detailed understanding of your target market, consider these elements:

1. **Irrationally passionate.** Identify niches where people are exceptionally passionate. For instance, consider the fitness market, particularly segments like CrossFit enthusiasts or yoga practitioners. These groups often invest significantly in their interests, from specialized equipment to membership fees and workshops.

2. **Great in number.** Focus on broad markets where the number of potential customers is vast. The beauty and skincare industry exemplifies this approach, with a wide range of demographics seeking products and advice. Another example is the tech gadget market, which appeals to a large and diverse consumer base.

3. **Easily accessible.** Determine markets that are easy to reach through available channels. Social media platforms like Instagram are ideal for reaching fashion and lifestyle markets, while LinkedIn is perfect for targeting professionals for services like career coaching or business-to-business (B2B) solutions.

4. **You enjoy serving.** Reflect on markets you would genuinely enjoy serving. If you have a background in music, targeting aspiring musicians or music enthusiasts could be fulfilling. Similarly, if you're

passionate about sustainable living, ecoconscious consumers could be a rewarding demographic.

5. **Combining parameters.** The ideal target market meets all four criteria. For example, pet owners often show irrational passion for pet-related products, form a large demographic, are easily reachable through dedicated pet forums and social media groups, and can be a joy to serve if you're an animal lover.

6. **Research and validate.** Once you've listed potential markets, validate them through research. Use tools like surveys, social media analytics, and market reports to understand the viability and size of these markets.

7. **Experiment.** Don't hesitate to test small before fully committing to a target market. Run pilot campaigns or offer introductory services to gauge response and refine your understanding.

8. **Adapt.** Be prepared to pivot if your chosen market doesn't respond as expected. Flexibility and responsiveness to market feedback are key in finding the right target market.

When you take this comprehensive approach, you can ensure a targeted, effective, and enjoyable business strategy—one that serves you as well as your ideal buyers.

How I Did This All Backwards (and It Still Worked Out)

Over twenty-five years ago, at the start of my career, I faced a daunting challenge: I discovered a solution that no one knew about for a problem that no one was talking about.

When I discovered *Success Anorexia,* a condition I both discovered and named, I realized that it was a hidden condition that leads to behaviors like self-sabotage, self-limiting beliefs, and holding yourself back from success.

Realizing that I had inadvertently solved a problem that most people weren't even aware of, I decided to craft a unique solution, which was originally called my *Permission to Succeed® System.* This approach wasn't just a set of steps; it was a transformative journey.

This became the bedrock of my teachings, evolving into later works like my Power Habits® System and my Afformations Advantage. My journey highlights a critical aspect of entrepreneurship: often our most significant breakthroughs come from solving the problems that we ourselves face, thereby resonating with a broader audience that experiences similar challenges.

Creating your 7-Figure Offers means identifying unique market problems and developing tailored solutions that will solve human problems. The journey of discovering and addressing Success Anorexia exemplifies the impact of such an approach, showcasing the power of transforming personal insights into universal solutions.

This strategy doesn't just provide a pathway to success; it paves the way for creating offers that will deeply connect with and transform the lives of your target audience, and will transform your life and business as well.

THE MORE YOU DELAY, THE MORE YOU'LL PAY.

However, it's crucial to remember what I talked about earlier in this book: *money loves speed*. One of the biggest enemies of speed is *perfectionism*. Waiting for the perfect moment or trying to create the perfect offer will stall your progress. The truth is, perfection is an illusion, especially in the fast-paced world of business. By striving for excellence rather than perfection, you can move forward more quickly, learning and improving as you go.

Now let's go to the next step in my 7-Figure Machine Framework.

2

My 7-Figure Product Secrets

Marketing isn't everything, but it's the only thing.

—NOAH ST. JOHN

In this chapter, we'll explore the crucial steps of product creation. I'll guide you from concept to realization. First, we'll begin by determining your target market, a foundational step that dictates the direction and nature of your product. Understanding who you're creating for is critical in aligning your product with market needs and preferences.

Next, I'll show you how to specify your ideal client, going beyond broad market definitions to pinpoint the exact profile of the individual who will benefit most from your product. This specificity ensures your product resonates deeply with your clients, addressing their unique challenges and desires.

Then I'll reveal how to decide on the type of product you want to create. This decision is influenced by both your market's needs and your personal strengths or preferences. Whether it's a digital course, a physical product, or a service, this step shapes the form and function of your final offering.

Lastly, I'll introduce you to my P.O.W.E.R. Formula, which will guide you through the product creation process. These secrets will help ensure that your product meets market demands and stands out in a crowded marketplace.

First, Specify Your Ideal Buyer

The first step to creating your first (or next) 7-figure product is to specify your ideal buyer. This is like setting the coordinates for a successful business journey. It's about understanding who will benefit the most from your product or service, ensuring that every aspect of your business, from product development to marketing, speaks directly to their needs and desires.

If you forget or neglect to clearly define your ideal buyer, it can lead to a scattershot approach, where your message gets lost in the noise, failing to engage any specific group effectively. This misalignment results in wasted resources, both in terms of time and money, and can lead to a product-market mismatch. Products may end up being too broad, not quite hitting the mark for anyone, leading to disappointing sales and growth figures.

Moreover, without a well-defined target buyer, scaling your business becomes a game of chance rather than strategy. You risk diluting your brand's identity and value proposition, making it harder to stand out in a competitive market. In contrast, a clear understanding of your ideal buyer paves the way for targeted, impactful, and successful business growth.

Here's how to specify your ideal buyer:

1. **Choose one target market.** Begin by narrowing your focus to a single, specific market. This concentrated approach allows for a deeper understanding of and connection with your audience's needs and desires.

2. **List key problems.** Identify the key frustrations and problems your target market faces. For instance, if you're targeting entrepreneurs, common issues might include burnout, inefficient processes, or lack of work-life balance. Understanding these pain points is crucial in crafting solutions that resonate with your ideal buyer.

3. **Identify desirable outcomes.** In addition to listing the pain points your ideal buyers want to avoid, you also need to outline the positive goals and results they aspire to achieve. For entrepreneurs, these might include increased productivity, more significant profits, or better time management.

4. **Understand past attempts and purchases.** Analyze what your target market has tried in the past to achieve their goals. This might include specific courses, tools, or consulting services. Understanding these choices helps you position your product as a unique and superior solution.

5. **Analyze the gap.** By comparing where your target market is (point 2) versus where they want to be (point 3), you can identify a gap that your product can fill.

6. **Tailor your solution.** Use the insights gained in the previous steps to tailor your product's features and benefits, ensuring they address the specific pains and aspirations identified.

7. **Feedback loop.** Engage with potential clients to validate your assumptions about their undesirable results and desired outcomes, refining your product concept.

8. **Finalize your client profile.** Using this comprehensive analysis, create a detailed

profile of your ideal client, which will guide your product development and marketing efforts. This detailed approach ensures that your product is aligned with the market's needs as well as being uniquely positioned to offer effective solutions.

Buyer-Focused versus Solution-Focused

When I discovered Success Anorexia and Afformations in 1997, I realized that I had discovered something that was unique in the personal development industry. I also realized that I had identified unique solutions to existing problems that millions of people had.

The trouble was that, because I didn't know anything about marketing or product development, I was groping in the dark for solutions. It also didn't help that all of the marketing gurus to whom I gave insane amounts of money couldn't teach their way out of a paper bag.

That's why it took me far too long to realize what I now share with my coaching clients—that it's far easier to come from a *buyer-focused* paradigm than a *solution-focused* paradigm.

Meaning, if I had followed the steps I'm giving you in this book and that I give my coaching clients from the beginning of my entrepreneurial journey, I'd probably be a gazillionaire by now!

However, as I often say to my clients: "My pain is *your* gain." The great news for you is that you don't have to make the same costly mistakes I did. Instead, learn from my example of what to do, as well as what not to do.

How to Choose Which Type of Product to Create

The next step to creating 7-figure products is deciding which kind of product you're going to create. Choosing the right product type is crucial for the success of your business, because it shapes your development path, defines your market engagement, and impacts how you're going to allocate your time, money, and attention.

The right product choice ensures that you efficiently cater to your target audience's needs, maximizing the impact and profitability of your business. On the flip side, a misjudged product decision can lead to significant financial loss, wasted resources, and a lack of market resonance, potentially derailing your business.

Therefore, carefully consider the type of product you want to create. This isn't just about matching your skills to the market demand; it's about setting a sustainable and profitable course for your business's future.

Here are the 7 main product types and the pros and cons of each:

Product Type 1: Book

A book is often the first choice for many aspiring experts, primarily because of its powerful impact in establishing credibility and authority. As a tangible demonstration of expertise, a well-crafted book can open numerous doors, laying the foundation for a broader business model that includes speaking engagements, courses, and coaching services.

This initial step in product creation can act as a keystone around which you can build a multifaceted, lucrative business, which also effectively sets the stage for long-term success and substantial revenue generation.

A BOOK CAN BE YOUR GATEWAY TO YOUR 7-FIGURE MACHINE.

Pros

1. **Demonstrates your expertise.** Books showcase your knowledge and establish you as an authority in your field.

2. **Wide reach and accessibility.** Books can be accessed globally, extending your influence and client base.

3. **Excellent marketing tool.** Books serve as an effective marketing tool, enhancing your brand and opening doors to speaking engagements, workshops, and other opportunities.

Cons

1. **High competition.** The market is saturated, making it challenging to stand out among numerous titles.

2. **Time-intensive.** Writing a quality book requires a significant investment of time and effort.

3. **Lower profit margins.** Due to production costs and market pricing standards, profit margins per book can be relatively low.

Creating your first (or next) book requires balancing these pros and cons to determine if this avenue aligns with your specific business goals and capabilities.

Example: See **NoahStJohn.com/books.**

Product Type 2: Online Course

Creating an online course is a fantastic way to take what you know and turn it into a profitable product. It's not just about sharing your expertise; it's about creating an engaging, educational journey for your audience. With online courses, you can reach people from all corners of the globe, offering your ideal buyers valuable skills and knowledge right where they are—which is why this is often referred to as "making money in your sleep."

AN ONLINE COURSE CAN MAKE YOU MONEY WHILE YOU SLEEP.

Pros

1. **Global reach.** Your course can be accessed by anyone, anywhere, breaking geographical barriers.
2. **Scalability.** Once created, it can be sold to an unlimited number of people without additional costs.
3. **Interactive learning experience.** Courses often include videos, quizzes, and other interactive elements that enhance the learning experience.

Cons

1. **Technical requirements.** Creating a high-quality online course requires technical know-how and potentially significant upfront investment in equipment or software.
2. **Market saturation.** The online course market can be highly competitive, with numerous courses on similar topics.
3. **Ongoing updates needed.** To keep your course relevant, you'll need to update it regularly as your field evolves.

Creating an online course is about striking the right balance between your expertise, market demand, and the unique value you can offer. If executed well, it's a journey that can lead to significant rewards in terms of both financial gain and the satisfaction of impacting lives globally.

Example: Explore my different online course offerings, like Power Habits® Academy, Get Unstuck Now, and The 7-Figure Machine, at **ShopNoahStJohn.com**.

Product Type 3: 5-Day Challenge

Launching a 5-day challenge (also known as a *virtual challenge*) is an exciting and dynamic way to engage with your audience. It's about creating a short, focused event that delivers quick wins and valuable insights. This format allows you to showcase your expertise and personality, helping your participants connect with you on a more personal level, which can then lead them to purchase higher-ticket programs from you, like coaching or Done for You Offers.

A 5-day challenge is designed to provide participants with a highly interactive and actionable learning experience over the course of five days. Each day focuses on a specific task or set of tasks, encouraging participants to take concrete steps towards achieving a particular goal.

This format is particularly effective because it creates a sense of urgency and community among participants, fostering engagement through daily activities, live sessions, or interactive content.

The primary objective of a 5-day challenge is to deliver immediate value to participants, showcasing your ability to produce results and establishing your authority in your field. By participating, attendees get a taste of what it's like to work with you, which can lead to increased interest in your higher-ticket offerings.

A 5-DAY CHALLENGE CAN GIVE YOU RAPID ENGAGEMENT AND IMMEDIATE RESULTS.

Pros

1. **High engagement.** Challenges create a buzz, encouraging active participation and fostering a sense of community.
2. **Immediate impact.** Short-term format delivers quick results, enhancing participant satisfaction.
3. **Brand visibility.** Boosts your visibility and helps in building your email list.

Cons

1. **Intensive planning.** Requires thorough planning and organization.
2. **Participant commitment.** Keeping participants engaged for five days can be challenging.
3. **Limited depth.** Its short duration only allows it to cover surface-level content.

Example: I offer a Power Habits® 5-Day Challenge, in which I teach people the habits that magnetically attract success and high-value opportunities, so they can break free from the cycle of unfulfilled potential, self-doubt, and lack of direction. Participants learn how to:

- Install key habits that exponentially grow business.
- Effortlessly drive more leads, sales, and profits daily.

- Stand out in any industry, enhancing professional longevity and client impact.

To learn more, visit **HabitsChallenge.com**.

Product Type 4: Virtual Event

A virtual event is an online gathering where business owners and professionals connect, learn, and engage in real time, right from their computers. Virtual events can open doors to immersive engagement, connecting you with a wider audience in real time. This format is particularly effective for expanding your reach and creating interactive, community-driven experiences that can lead to higher-ticket sales.

VIRTUAL EVENTS CAN GIVE YOU GLOBAL ENGAGEMENT WITHOUT THE HASSLE OF TRAVEL.

Pros

1. **Enhances engagement.** Creates an interactive environment that encourages participant involvement.

2. **Builds community.** Fosters a sense of connection and community among attendees.

3. **Increases brand exposure.** Broadens your reach, enhancing your brand's visibility without the expense of travel.

Cons

1. **Resource-intensive.** Demands significant planning, coordination, and technical setup.
2. **Time zone challenges.** Accommodating global audiences can be tricky in terms of local times.
3. **Participant retention.** Keeping attendees engaged throughout the event can be challenging.

While virtual events demand considerable planning and technological setup, their unique ability to connect, engage, and inspire a global audience from the comfort of their homes makes them an increasingly popular and effective tool for business owners. These events not only enhance your brand's visibility but also create a dynamic platform for knowledge sharing and community building, offering a versatile and impactful way to reach and resonate with your ideal buyers.

Product Type 5: Group Coaching

Group coaching is a dynamic format where the coach (you) works with multiple clients simultaneously, typically focusing on a common theme or goal. This approach combines personalized guidance with the benefits of learning from peers, creating a collaborative and interactive environment. Group coaching is excellent for sharing experiences, gaining new perspectives, and fostering a supportive community.

Group coaching stands out as a powerful tool in your 7-Figure Machine, because it combines the benefits of individual attention with the rich, diverse insights of a group setting. It fosters a collaborative learning environment and cultivates a sense of community, enhancing the overall coaching experience. This method, with its unique balance of shared and individual growth, offers a compelling way to engage and develop clients, making it an invaluable part of any coaching portfolio.

GROUP COACHING HELPS YOU LEVERAGE YOUR TIME AND ENERGY.

Pros

1. **Efficient use of resources.** Coaches can impact multiple clients in one session, optimizing time and effort.

2. **Peer learning.** Participants benefit from one another's insights and experiences.

3. **Cost-effective for clients.** Group coaching is typically more affordable than one-on-one coaching, making it accessible to a broader audience.

Cons

1. **Less personalization.** Individual attention is limited compared to one-on-one coaching.
2. **Group dynamics.** Managing different personalities and ensuring equal participation can be challenging.
3. **Varying progress rates.** Participants may progress at different rates, which requires careful management.

Example: I offer a 12-week group coaching program called **The 12-Week Breakthrough** where I teach a group of entrepreneurs the exact roadmap to scale your business effortlessly so financial freedom becomes your new norm. Participants in this program discover:

- How to find, discover, and use your own personal superpower so you can dominate your niche (and that's only the second-best benefit).
- A megavaluable way to create unbreakable habits and shatter your limitations.

- The final piece of the success puzzle. Skipping this will create a monster-sized problem for your growth trajectory.
- The horrible mistake most entrepreneurs make when it comes to time management.
- The nasty procrastination trap and how to make it disappear so you can achieve your wildest dreams.
- How to crank out innovative solutions as easily as falling off a log.
- Within you slumbers a titan of industry. I'll show you how to wake it up.
- How to deal with setbacks like a Zen master and blow away the competition.
- A way to leverage your network so easily you'll think I'm pulling your leg (until you see the results).
- How to escape the pure gut-wrenching agony of financial instability.
- Gain insider access by going through this "back door" (a true, actual shortcut to scaling your business).

If you're looking for these kinds of results in your business, schedule a complimentary Breakthrough Consultation and apply for admission to The 12-Week Breakthrough at **BreakthroughwithNoah.com.**

Product Type 6: One-on-One Coaching

One-on-one coaching is a highly focused and personalized approach in which you dedicate your full attention to an individual client. With this method, you tailor your coaching experience to address specific goals, challenges, and personal development needs. This environment fosters strong, trust-based connections and facilitates in-depth exploration, paving the way for profound personal and professional growth.

One-on-one coaching stands at the pinnacle of personalized development, offering profound opportunities for growth and transformation. Its direct focus makes it an incredibly effective tool for achieving significant personal and professional milestones. This coaching style, with its deep dive into individual challenges and aspirations, remains a cornerstone of impactful coaching practices.

Offering both one-on-one and group coaching is a strategic approach that allows you to cater to diverse client needs and preferences, maximizing your revenue potential. One-on-one coaching offers the advantage of deep, personalized guidance, enabling you to charge premium rates for the exclusive attention and customized solutions you provide. On the other hand, group coaching leverages your time more efficiently, allowing you to serve more clients simultaneously at a lower individual cost.

This blend ensures a balanced portfolio, where the high-touch, high-value nature of personal coaching complements the scalability of group sessions. By providing both options, you can attract a wider range of clients, from those seeking an intimate coaching experience to those who benefit from the dynamics and affordability of a group setting, ultimately increasing your earning potential and impact. That's why I offer both group and one-on-one coaching: in order to provide the most valuable service to the widest range of clients.

The highly personal nature of one-on-one coaching often leads to the most profound, life-changing transformations for clients. For example, executive one-on-one coaching has enabled many of my greatest client transformations to take place—from Charles adding $1.8 million in 10 months to Adam growing his company's revenues from $4 million to $20 million in less than 18 months. Both of these represent instances where the highly focused nature of one-on-one coaching led to dramatic, life-changing results for my clients.

ONE-ON-ONE COACHING ALLOWS YOU TO COMMAND HIGHER FEES.

Pros

1. **Personalized attention.** Offers in-depth, customized coaching specific to the client's needs.

2. **Flexibility in approach.** Can adapt techniques and strategies to suit individual learning styles and goals.

3. **Higher fees.** Because of the highly personalized nature of one-on-one coaching, you can typically command higher fees.

Cons

1. **Time-intensive.** Requires significant time commitment per client, limiting the number of clients you can handle at any given time.

2. **Emotional and mental investment.** The depth of personal involvement required can be demanding for some coaches.

3. **Market limitations.** While this approach is lucrative, the market size for high-ticket coaching is generally smaller compared to more affordable group programs or digital products.

Example: For a detailed description and application for one-on-one coaching with me, visit **NoahMentor.com**.

Product Type 7: Done for You Services

Done for You services involve taking complete responsibility for a particular task or project on behalf of a client. This service is ideal for clients looking for expert solutions without the need to be involved in the process. As I discussed in the previous chapter, these are high-value offerings that directly translate your expertise into tangible results for your clients.

Done for You services present an opportunity to deliver exceptional value while achieving lucrative returns. By offering these tailored solutions, you not only meet specific client needs but cement your reputation as a leader in your industry.

> **DONE FOR YOU SERVICES CAN BE HIGHLY LUCRATIVE.**

Pros

1. **High revenue potential.** Attracts high-ticket clients, offering significant financial returns.

2. **Expert positioning.** Reinforces your status as an expert in your field.

3. **Client satisfaction.** High level of client satisfaction due to the comprehensive nature of the service.

Cons

1. **Resource-intensive.** Requires a significant investment of time and expertise.
2. **Scalability limitations.** More challenging to scale compared to digital products or group programs.
3. **Client dependency.** Risk of becoming overly reliant on a few high-value clients.

Examples: My Book Done for You and Funnel Done for You Services provide a streamlined path to success, removing the overwhelm of creating your own book or sales funnel. With these services, you benefit from expertly crafted content and strategic book and funnel design, ensuring your message reaches your audience effectively and converts leads into loyal clients, all while saving you precious time and energy. See: **NoahStJohn.com/doneforyou** and **NoahStJohn.com/ bookdoneforyou** for more information.

Key Points to Consider

1. You can create more than one product, but you should focus on creating only one product at a time. Otherwise, you'll probably get overwhelmed—which will likely cause you to quit before you finish.

2. I've listed the pros and cons of each type of product so you can decide which one to focus on first. There's no perfect product; as you can see from the discussion above, each one has its pros and cons. That's why I've decided to have a mix of all of them for my company, SuccessClinic.com.

3. Be sure to check out the examples that I've given you of each type of product so you can see different examples of each.

4. I started with one book, and now I have an entire product suite, which includes group coaching, one-on-one coaching, and Done for You services. What this means for you is unparalleled access to a comprehensive ecosystem of support and resources designed to elevate your success. Whether you're seeking personalized guidance, collaborative learning environments, or turnkey solutions, my suite of offerings caters to diverse needs and learning styles, ensuring you have the tools and strategies to achieve your goals efficiently and effectively.

Create Your Signature Transformation Model

The next step to creating your 7-Figure product is creating your Signature Transformation Model

(STM). Your STM refers to a distinctive, personalized framework or methodology developed by an expert or coach in their field. This encapsulates your unique approach to solving specific problems or helping your ideal buyer achieve their goals.

You want to come up with a brand name that reflects your product's uniqueness and differentiates it from other methods in the market. This can often become a cornerstone of your identity. It provides a structured way for clients to engage with your philosophy and techniques.

For example, I enjoy creating new methods that solve age-old problems. Some of the Signature Transformation Models that I'm known for include:

- **The Afformations® Advantage:** A new way to overcome negative thinking and turn self-limiting beliefs into self-empowering behaviors.
- **The Power Habits® System.** A new approach to solve the age-old problem of self-sabotage and holding yourself back from success.
- **iAfform® Audios.** A new way to turn negative beliefs into positive action while you're not even paying attention.
- **The 7-Figure Machine.** A new way to solve the business owner's number one problem: not making enough money to justify all the hard work and long hours they're putting in.

- **The 7-Figure Expert Formula.** A new way to scale your expert business without stress or overwhelm.
- **My Get Unstuck Now Framework.** A fresh approach to the problem of being stuck.

You don't have to create as many STMs as I have in order to have a 7- or even 8-figure business. In fact, many of my clients have added multiple 6 figures and more with just one new solution to an old problem.

I LOVE CREATING NEW SOLUTIONS TO OLD PROBLEMS.

Why is it so important to create your own STM? Because if you don't, you're going to get lost in a sea of sameness. It's not just about offering a solution; it's about creating an innovative approach to a common problem. For example, remember when Beachbody came out with the P90X home fitness programs and their infomercials were everywhere? They came up with the term "muscle confusion" and in their advertising hammered home the point that you're not losing weight because you're not spending hours in the gym; it's because you're not confusing your muscles!

But what actually is "muscle confusion"? Answer: exercise! It was simply a brilliant repackaging of something that's existed for decades, explained in a very clever way.

THIS WAS ONE OF THE BEST EXAMPLES I'VE EVER SEEN.

In short, an effective STM goes beyond solving problems; it reimagines the solution, making your brand synonymous with innovation and quality, much like successful companies that have transformed their sectors with groundbreaking approaches.

Here are ten other examples of successful companies or products that have stood out by creating unique solutions to common problems:

1. **Apple's iPhone**. Revolutionized the mobile phone industry with its unique design and user interface.
2. **Tesla's electric cars**. Redefined the automotive industry with sustainable, high-performance electric vehicles.
3. **Airbnb**. Transformed the lodging industry with a new approach to short-term rentals.
4. **Netflix**. Changed home entertainment by introducing streaming services.
5. **Amazon's Kindle**. Innovated the reading experience with digital ebook technology.
6. **Spotify**. Reshaped music consumption with its streaming service and personalized playlists.

7. **Uber.** Altered the transportation sector with its app-based ride-hailing service.

8. **Dollar Shave Club.** Disrupted the grooming industry with a subscription-based model.

9. **GoPro.** Created a new category in photography with its action cameras.

10. **Warby Parker.** Revolutionized the eyewear industry with a direct-to-consumer model and virtual try-on technology.

Each of these companies created a unique solution that addressed existing problems in innovative ways, setting new industry standards and gaining a competitive edge. In a marketplace where innovation and distinctiveness are key, an STM is not just an advantage; it's a necessity for long-term success.

How to Create Your STM
Step 1: Deeply Describe the Specific Problem You're Solving

Identifying the specific problem your product solves is the cornerstone of creating an effective Signature Transformation Model. This step requires a deep understanding of your target audience and the challenges they face.

In this step, you need to pinpoint a specific problem that is significant, pervasive, and resonates strongly with your ideal buyers. The problem should align with your expertise and the unique solutions you can provide.

There's an old saying in marketing: "If you can describe your prospect's problem better than they can, your sale is 80 percent made." That's one reason why products like P90X were so successful—because the people watching their infomercials would go, "Yes, that's me!" when the problem was described (in this case, spending hours at the gym and still not losing weight).

DESCRIBE YOUR BUYER'S PROBLEM BETTER THAN THEY CAN.

In addition, by focusing on a specific problem (for example, you're holding yourself back from the level of success you're capable of) rather than a general one (you want to make more money), your STM gains relevance and urgency, making it a compelling and necessary intervention for your audience. This clear identification sets the stage for developing a transformative solution that addresses the problem effectively, as well as positioning your STM as an indispensable tool.

Step 2: Twist the Knife

While it might sound gruesome, "twisting the knife" in your STM means intensifying the urgency of the problem you're addressing. In this step, you vividly illustrate the negative consequences if the problem remains unsolved, such as missed opportunities, continued struggles, or worsening issues.

Conversely, it's crucial to highlight the positive outcomes of addressing the problem—the possibilities that open up, the growth that can be achieved, and the success stories of those who have already made this transformation. In this step, you don't simply present the facts; you must emotionally engage your audience, making the problem and the solution deeply relatable and compelling.

PEOPLE BUY BECAUSE THEY'RE IN PAIN.

Incorporating case studies here and providing specific examples of transformation and success can powerfully demonstrate the real-life impact of your STM. For example, when I do this step, I often give specific, real-life examples of my coaching clients whom I've helped. Here is one approach I use:

Because of coaching with me:

- Misty made $150,000 in eight weeks.
- Mike doubled his income *twice* in twelve weeks.
- Britnie created a $40 million success story and now owns her own island in the Caribbean.
- Kathryn raised over $115,000 in private money in one day.
- Tim built a 7-figure home-based business in less than 2 years
- Brian made an extra $95,000 in commissions in less than twelve *days*.
- Steven's business grew 800 percent in 12 weeks.
- Sheila's sales went from $5,000 per month to $75,000 per month in less than six months.
- Bill went from struggling to doing multibillion-dollar real estate deals.
- Kathy's sales doubled in just nine weeks.
- George went from 80-hour work weeks to 6-figure months and married the love of his life.

You can see many more examples on my websites like **BreakthroughwithNoah.com**. When you share real-life case studies like these, your prospect will be far more likely to feel confident in hiring you, because they'll be likely to think, "Gee, if Noah's program got results like that for all those people, imagine what it could do for me!"

That's why health and money are the easiest "before and after" stories to share. For example, it's easy to see the difference between when a customer was overweight before your program to where they're in great shape as a result of your program.

It's also easy to see the difference between when a client was stuck or struggling before taking my coaching to where they're making more money as a result of coaching with me.

IMAGINE WHAT THIS COULD DO FOR YOU.

It's also important to highlight speed (*this* outcome in *this* short amount of time), because no one wants to wait to see results. However, while everyone wants overnight success, it's also important to highlight the fact that these transformations are the result of following the system and putting in the work—not waving a magic wand. (This will also discourage the tire kickers and freebie seekers who expect results to magically occur.)

Step 3: Present Your Custom Branded Solution

The next step is to present your Custom Branded Solution (CBS). This is where your unique value proposition shines brightest. A CBS isn't just a solution; it's a brand experience, wrapped in your unique perspective and methodology.

This means showcasing how your approach is not just different, but more effective than your competitor's solutions. Your CBS should reflect your brand's core values and strengths, making it resonate deeply with your target audience.

This solution needs to be more than a service; it should feel like a journey that your clients embark on with you, one that is packed with transformative potential and unmatched expertise.

DIFFERENT IS BETTER THAN BETTER.

Every aspect of your CBS, from its name to its execution, must speak the language of your brand, telling a story that aligns with your clients' aspirations and challenges. This isn't just about solving a problem; it's about creating a memorable, engaging experience that positions you as the go-to expert in your field. Some of the most striking and famous instances in recent history not only created unique identities but revolutionized their industries. For example:

- **Steve Jobs.** Redefined mobile technology as an all-in-one device (the iPhone); disrupted the communication market.

- **Elon Musk.** Pioneered sustainable, high-performance electric vehicles (Tesla); disrupted the automobile market.
- **Airbnb.** Introduced a novel concept for short-term, home-based rentals; disrupted the hotel industry.
- **Netflix.** Shifted entertainment to online streaming from physical rentals; disrupted home entertainment.
- **Uber.** Revolutionized transportation with app-based ride-hailing; disrupted the travel industry.
- **Warby Parker.** Changed eyewear with direct-to-consumer sales and virtual try-ons; disrupted the eyewear industry.

Now you might be saying, "But Noah, I'm not Steve Jobs or Elon Musk!" Well, neither am I. I know all too well how hard it is to come up with new solutions to old problems. However, as entrepreneur Mark Cuban has often said, "You just need one."

You don't have to disrupt the entire industry you're in, whether it's health, wealth, or relationships. You just need to create something that your ideal buyer hasn't heard before, or else you're just going to get lost in a sea of sameness. There's simply no market that isn't oversaturated at this point, so how are you going to get customers and clients if your solution is the same as everyone else's?

That's why I spend a lot of time and attention helping my group coaching and one-on-one clients create their Signature Transformation Models and Custom Branded Solutions: because without these arrows in your marketing quiver, you're going to be shooting blanks (yes, I know I just mixed my metaphors).

Step 4. Follow My PRODUCT Formula

Your final step to creating a powerful, transformational product is my PRODUCT Formula, a cutting-edge approach designed to create powerful and transformational products. This methodology is more than just a checklist; it's a comprehensive guide to developing offerings that resonate deeply with your target audience and deliver tangible, transformative results.

Each letter in my PRODUCT Formula represents a crucial element in crafting a product that not only meets but exceeds customer expectations. This formula encapsulates the essence of what makes a product not just good, but great—ensuring that every aspect, from conception to delivery, aligns with the highest standards of quality and effectiveness.

1. **Precision.** Your product should offer a specific solution tailored to a narrowly defined audience, ensuring relevance and effectiveness.

2. **Result.** Focus on delivering one significant promise rather than multiple minor ones, enhancing clarity and impact.

3. **Objective.** Align your product with the core desires of your target market, speaking directly to their needs and aspirations.

4. **Delivery.** Prioritize immediate solutions, providing prompt gratification and results to your customers.

5. **Upscale.** Design your product to nurture future business opportunities, setting the stage for a lasting customer relationship.

6. **Caliber.** Ensure your product's presentation is professional and high-quality, enhancing its perceived value.

7. **Truth.** Deliver on your promises with genuine assistance and value, building trust and credibility.

Let me give you examples of each step of my PRODUCT Formula across many different industries:

1. **Precision.** An app designed specifically for remote workers to enhance productivity, focusing solely on this audience's unique needs.

2. **Result.** A weight loss program that promises and delivers a significant health transformation within a 90-day period.

3. **Objective.** A financial planning service targeting retirees, addressing their specific goal of maximizing retirement savings.

4. **Delivery.** An online course offering immediate access to learning materials and quick-start guides for fast implementation.

5. **Upscale.** A beginner's photography workshop that introduces participants to a more advanced, ongoing master class series.

6. **Caliber.** A luxury skincare line that not only delivers exceptional results but is also packaged and presented in a high-end, aesthetically pleasing manner.

7. **Truth.** A personal coaching service where clients consistently achieve their set goals, showcasing genuine effectiveness.

In case you're wondering how to use case studies, here's an example from Aubrey, one of my coaching clients:

When I first attended a Noah St. John event, I came thinking, "How can Noah figure out things about me? I'm different than anyone else, and I don't think these things will come up." But the things Noah says bring up ideas and thoughts in your mind to where you learn that much more about yourself.

Now everybody comes from different walks of life, different businesses, different issues, different things that they're stuck in, different head trash, as Noah calls it. And he has a way of engaging everybody. It doesn't matter where you're stuck, I'm able to learn more and grow more. Before you even realize it, he's taught you how to make more money and you don't even realize how it happened! I know that happened with me. And it was simply before I even really started working his habits into my business, it was really getting rid of the head trash as he teaches. And as I did that, *within a year, my business income that I had actually had for 15 years had DOUBLED* simply by incorporating the habits that Noah teaches.

The fact is, there's no better time than right now. It seems inconvenient initially, but then once you've done it, you're like, "I can't imagine having missed that and not having that peace in my life."

Have you heard of the phrase "working yourself to death"? Aubrey had been doing that before she came to me. It's true: she told me that she had been working at 100 or more hours every week for *15 years.* 15 years!

She was working so hard that she ended up in a wheelchair, and her doctors told her that she might never walk again. They told her that she had to stop working so hard. But she couldn't, because she was on a treadmill and working, working, working all the time.

AUBREY WAS LITERALLY WORKING HERSELF TO DEATH.

When Aubrey first came to one of my events, she was at her lowest point. Yet because of my coaching and her implementation, *she doubled her income in just 12 months, after 15 years of nearly working herself to death.*

Many people will read Aubrey's story and the other case studies in this book or on my website and say to themselves, "Sure, they did it, but it won't work for me."

Guess what? If you believe this won't work for you, you're right!

However, if you believe this can and will work for you, you're right about that too.

Henry Ford is quoted as saying, "Whether you believe you can or can't, you're right."

With all due respect to Mr. Ford, I have updated that quote to the following: Whether you believe you can or you believe you can't, you *make yourself* right.

That's why, when you read the real-life case studies of my one-on-one or group coaching clients in this book or on my websites, I want you to start saying this:

WHETHER YOU BELIEVE YOU CAN OR YOU BELIEVE YOU CAN'T, YOU *MAKE YOURSELF* RIGHT.

If they did it, why not me?

Let me ask you a question: Is it ridiculous to think that just one thing I've taught you so far in this book could help you get better results in the next 12 weeks?

I hope you agree that it's not ridiculous at all. In fact, it's perfectly logical, right?

Here's All You Need to Succeed

The only three things you need to succeed are . . .

1. The right PLAN (what to do)
2. The right TOOLS (how to do it)
3. The right SUPPORT (the people who believe in you)

Building your dream business, dream career, and dream lifestyle is like building your dream home. First, you need the right PLAN: the blueprint you're going to follow.

In my one-on-one and group coaching programs, that's the paint-by-numbers, fill-in-the-blanks, plug-and-play systems, templates, resources, and strategies that have made me and my clients billions over the last two decades plus.

Then you need the right TOOLS, which enable you to actually build the business or lifestyle you desire.

Finally, you need the right SUPPORT. You need a person or people in your corner believing in you—oftentimes, before you even believe in yourself!

In my one-on-one and group coaching programs like The 12-Week Breakthrough, we call these The Three Pillars of Transformation: the right plan, the right tools, and the right support, so you reach your pot of gold faster than you ever could by working alone.

THE MORE YOU POSTPONE, THE LESS YOU'LL OWN.

Let me add a reminder that a goal without inspired action is just a dream. That means, you can have all the big dreams in the world—but if you don't act, nothing will happen! Don't fall victim to fear, procrastination, or perfectionism: three of your greatest enemies to wealth and fulfillment. Take inspired action in the face of fear, and you'll see your fortunes turn around more quickly than you ever thought possible.

Let me end this chapter with a quote from actor Denzel Washington:

I've found that nothing in life is worthwhile unless you take risks. Nothing. Nelson Mandela said, "There is no passion to be found playing small and settling for a life that's less than the one you're capable of living." Without consistency, you'll never finish. So do what you feel passionate about. Take chances. Don't be afraid to fail big, to dream big. But remember, dreams without goals are just dreams.

In our next chapter, I'll walk you through the next step in my 7-Figure Machine framework. Let's go!

3

My 7-Figure Cash Machine Secrets

Measure twice, cut once.

—BUILDER'S CREDO

As I've already mentioned, I grew up poor in a rich neighborhood: Kennebunkport, Maine. We lived in a drafty, unfinished home that my parents lost to foreclosure when I was just fifteen years old.

That's why, growing up, I was painfully exposed to the chasm between the haves and have-nots: the haves were everyone else in the community, and the have-nots were my family.

Have you ever heard motivational speakers go on stage and say something like, "We were poor, but we were happy, so we didn't know we were poor"?

Well, in my family, we freaking knew we were poor—because my mother, bless her heart, reminded us every day that we were poor and miserable. So no, it wasn't happy—it sucked.

I also hated being poor because I saw that right down the street, there was great wealth and abundance. I was constantly thinking about money, because we didn't have any. I also saw the unfairness of money, because my parents worked hard yet never had any money; yet it seemed like the people who had lots of money didn't work all that hard. And that didn't make any sense to me.

Another thing that never made any sense to me was this idea of getting a job, working for forty years, and then being allowed to finally enjoy your life when you're too old to enjoy it. Yet that's the very thing that most of us were taught growing up. Our parents and teachers taught us that if we worked hard, got good grades, went to college, and got a good job, that we would be successful, and that would make us happy.

For some people, that worked just fine; but for me and many others, it didn't work at all. For example, when I got my first jobs in my teens and early twenties, I remember getting this tiny little paycheck twice a month. In fact, at one of my first paying jobs, I went to my manager at the time, showed her my paycheck, and said, "There must be some mistake, because . . . where's all my money?"

She explained that they have to take out taxes and Social Security and blah blah blah, and that was why what's left was next to nothing. And I remember thinking, "This is what I get to look forward to for the next forty years?"

That's one reason I decided to commit suicide at age twenty-five: I simply didn't want to live like that, and I didn't see any way out. Thankfully, my life was spared at the last moment, because in 1997, I finally found my life's purpose when I discovered Success Anorexia, the Power Habits System, and my Afformations Advantage.

I COULDN'T ACCEPT THAT THIS WAS MY FATE.

How to Make Money

There are many ways to make money, yet there are only a few ways to become wealthy. The most common way to make money is to get a job. A job is typically where you put in a certain amount of time in exchange for a certain amount of money.

For example, in my teens and early twenties, I held a series of what I call "survival jobs" because that was all I was able to do—merely survive. I worked long hours and got paid minimum wage, and that barely enabled me to pay for the basic necessities of food, clothing, and shelter. I had to work these jobs partly because I didn't have the education or qualifications to work higher-paying jobs.

In any event, a typical job is where you give a block of time in exchange for a block of money. Naturally, some jobs pay more than others because of their perceived value. According to Investopedia, here are the 10 highest-paying jobs in the United States and their average annual salaries:

- Cardiologist: $353,970
- Anesthesiologist: $331,190
- Oral and maxillofacial surgeon: $311,460
- Emergency medicine physician: $310,640
- Orthopedic surgeon (except pediatric): $306,220
- Dermatologist: $302,740
- Radiologist: $301,720
- Surgeon (other): $297,800
- Obstetrician-gynecologist: $296,210
- Pediatric surgeon: $290,310

Every single one of these high-paying jobs requires years of medical school, which for most people also means hundreds of thousands of dollars in student loans.

Frankly, I admire anyone who decides to dedicate years of their life to studying and practicing medicine. However, from a very young age, I knew that was not the path that I wanted. In fact, because I was labeled a "gifted and talented" kid, my mother wanted me to either become a doctor or a lawyer. Yet neither of those professions held any interest to me whatsoever.

Can you relate? Have you ever found yourself working at a job and thought, "Is this all there is?" In my more than twenty-five years of coaching 7- and 8-figure CEOs, entrepreneurs, and executives, I've found that almost all of them had an aha! moment like mine, when they realized that the "normal" path that most of us were taught was simply not for them. That was why they started their business in the first place.

I also hated having a job because I felt I didn't own my own life. I felt as if someone else was controlling my future and my destiny, and I didn't like that. Of course, the good thing about having a job is "security," but I put that word in quotation marks because most of us know how fleeting the "security" of a job actually is. Most of us know of someone, or have personally experienced, working at a job for years and suddenly being let go. This means that no matter how good you are or how long you've worked there, someone else is in charge of your financial results.

None of that sat well with me, because I wanted to be in charge of my own financial destiny and make the decisions for my life. Whether I succeeded or failed, I wanted it to be because of decisions I made, not decisions that someone else made for me.

How to Become Wealthy

While I've just shown you how to make money, it took me a long time to realize that there's a very big difference between making money with a job and becoming wealthy. In fact, one of the only ways to become truly wealthy is to *sever the connection between time and money.*

THIS IS THE HIDDEN SECRET TO BECOMING TRULY WEALTHY.

In a typical job, you give one block of your time in exchange for a certain block of money. For example, you might work for forty hours in exchange for a paycheck at the end of the week. While there's nothing inherently wrong with that, the problem for me was that I couldn't see the endgame. I did the math and realized that if I kept doing that, I would never become financially free.

When you follow my 7-Figure Machine framework, you can sever the connection between time and money. This means that you can work for a block of time (whether it's an hour, a day, or a week) and get paid for that work until the end of time.

Let's say you follow my framework and create an online product, as I showed you in the previous chapter. The wonderful thing about having an online product is that you can build it once and sell it over and over until the end of time. That means, you put in one block of work and time, yet you can receive money from that same block over and over again, for as long as you like.

In fact, I've been helping entrepreneurs, experts, and executives to sever the connection between time and money for more than twenty-five years.

Of course, it takes an investment of time, money and energy up front in order to see a significant return. Yet I know of no other investment that yields such high returns!

Building Your Cash Machine Website

When I launched my online company SuccessClinic .com in 1997, the tools that were available for the average online entrepreneur were very limited and quite rudimentary by today's standards. Yet that's what we had to work with, so I had to find a way to make it work.

Since then, I've seen that there are three kinds of entrepreneurs who come to me. See which of these three categories you fit into:

1. You have a website that's bringing in good money.
2. You have a website, but it's not bringing in enough (or any) money yet.
3. You don't have a website yet.

Which of these categories do you fit into?

Since you're reading this book right now, I'm going to assume that you fall into either category 2 or 3: either your website isn't bringing in the amount of money you want, or you don't have a website yet.

Whichever category you find yourself in right now, let me introduce you to what I call my Hub & Spoke Method to Make Money Online. You can also call this your Building Your Cash Machine Website because when you get this right, you'll have created a method of bringing in money that will enable you to sever the connection between time and money.

In addition, I'm going to give you specific examples from my own business—which is how you can tell that my coaching is different from those marketing gurus who tell you to do one thing while doing something completely different!

Your Website: The Hub

When you visit my website **SuccessClinic.com**, you'll notice that it has a lot of pages—and when I say a lot of pages, I mean a *lot* of pages. You might look at that and say, "But Noah, I don't have the time to build all those pages!"

The great news for you is that there are only five pages you need to make really good money online. I call these the Foundational Five Pages of Your Cash Machine Website. They are:

1. **Your Home page.** Where you introduce yourself to the world.

2. **Your About page.** Where you tell your story of why you do what you do.

3. **Your Products and Services page.** Where you show what you have for sale.

4. **Your Blog.** Where you create articles and videos for search engine optimization (SEO): that is, drawing people to your website when they are searching for specific words or phrases.

5. **Your Contact Us page:** Where people can contact you.

"That's it, Noah?"

Yep, that's it!

Now let me walk you through each one of these Foundational Five in turn.

Foundational Page 1: Your Home Page

Your home page serves as the digital front door to your brand and business. This page should immediately capture your visitor's attention and succinctly convey who you are and what you offer.

Key elements include a compelling headline that encapsulates your unique value proposition, an engaging introduction that connects with your audience, and clear, direct calls to action guiding visitors to explore further. Avoid cluttering the page with too much information. Instead, focus on a clean, user-friendly design that guides visitors naturally through your content.

Use high-quality images and a professional layout to establish credibility and trust. First impressions matter immensely in the digital world, so ensure your home page reflects the essence of your brand and the value you provide.

On your home page, focus especially on these four critical elements:

1. **Headline.** Your home page needs a powerful and clear headline that grabs attention and

succinctly communicates what you offer. This could be a tagline, a brief statement of your unique value proposition, or a question that resonates with your target audience. Ensure that it's concise and speaks directly to the visitor's needs or problems.

2. **Visuals and layout.** Use high-quality visuals that align with your brand and message. A clean and intuitive layout helps visitors navigate your site easily. Incorporate elements like a hero image or a video that introduces you or your services. (A hero image is a large, attention-grabbing picture with text typically shown in the above-the-fold area of the webpage, directly beneath the website header.) Typically, a hero image takes up practically the whole pre-scroll full-width area on the page. Avoid overcrowding the page with too much text or too many images, which can overwhelm visitors and dilute your message.

3. **Content and messaging.** Include a brief introduction about who you are and what you do, emphasizing how you can help your visitors. This section should be engaging and relatable, encouraging visitors to explore more. Avoid using jargon or overly complex language. Be clear, straightforward, and personable.

4. **Call to action (CTA).** Your home page should guide visitors to take a specific action, whether it's to learn more about your services, sign up for a newsletter, or view your product offerings. CTAs should be prominent and clear—ideally placed above the fold for immediate visibility. Avoid vague or multiple CTAs that can cause confusion.

Your home page sets the tone for your entire website, so be sure to make it impactful, professional, and aligned with your overall brand strategy. In addition, this page will get the vast majority of traffic and visitors, so make sure it conveys the brand messaging you want to show to the world.

Example: NoahStJohn.com.

Foundational Page 2: Your About Page

Your About page is where you share your personal or company's story, detailing why you do what you do. This page is critical for building a connection with your audience and establishing trust. It should include:

1. **Personal journey.** Share your background and the path that led you to where you are today. This helps create a human connection.

2. **Mission and values.** Explain what drives you or your company, highlighting your core values and mission statement.

3. **Professional accomplishments.** Mention relevant achievements, experiences, and milestones that establish your credibility in your field.

4. **Personal elements.** Inject personal anecdotes or interests that humanize you or your company, fostering relatability.

5. **Engaging narrative.** Craft your content as a narrative that's engaging and easy to follow. Avoid overly formal or technical language.

6. **Visual elements.** Include professional photos or videos that complement your story and add a personal touch.

Your About page isn't just about listing qualifications; it's about telling a compelling story that resonates with your audience and gives insight into who you are and why you're passionate about what you do.

Example: NoahStJohn.com/our-story

Foundational Page 3: Your Products and Services Page

This page showcases your offerings and is crucial for converting visitors into customers. Key elements include:

1. **Clear descriptions.** Provide detailed, easy-to-understand descriptions of each product or service. Highlight benefits and features.

2. **Visual appeal.** Use high-quality images or videos to visually represent your offerings. This adds credibility and helps visitors understand what they're buying.

3. **Easy navigation.** Organize products/services clearly. Categories or filters help visitors find what they need quickly.

4. **Testimonials and reviews.** Share customer testimonials or reviews to build trust and provide social proof.

5. **Strong calls to action (CTAs).** Guide visitors to purchase or inquire further. Ensure that CTAs are clear and compelling.

This page should not only list your offerings but also communicate their value and how they solve the visitor's problems or meet their needs. I will talk more about this when we get to the "Spokes" section of your Cash Machine Website.

Example: NoahStJohn.com/shop.

Foundational Page 4: Your Blog

Your blog is an essential component of your website for driving organic traffic and establishing your authority in your niche. When done correctly, it can significantly boost your SEO efforts. Here's a detailed breakdown:

1. **Purpose and value.** Your blog should offer valuable, relevant content to your audience. This includes informative articles, how-to guides, and videos that solve problems or answer questions related to your industry.

2. **Common mistakes.** Many businesses fail by treating their blog as an afterthought, posting irregularly or only self-promotional content. This approach can turn off potential customers and diminish SEO benefits.

3. **SEO optimization.** Each blog post should be optimized for search engines. Use relevant keywords, but avoid keyword stuffing. Include metatitles, descriptions, and alt text for images. Metatitles are concise HTML elements that

define the title of a webpage and help search engines understand its content for SEO purposes. Alt text are textual descriptions assigned to images on a webpage to provide alternative information when the image cannot be displayed, aiding accessibility and helping search engines understand the image's content for SEO.

4. **Engagement and updates.** Regularly update your blog with fresh content. Engage with your audience by encouraging comments and sharing your posts on social media platforms.

5. **Quality over quantity.** Focus on creating high-quality content that provides value. It's better to have fewer, well-written posts than numerous low-quality ones.

6. **Analytics.** Use analytics to understand what content resonates with your audience. This data can guide your future content strategy.

Your blog is not just a platform to showcase your expertise, but also a tool to connect and build trust with your audience. It should reflect your brand's voice and provide consistent value to your readers.

Example: NoahStJohn.com/blog.

Foundational Page 5:
Your Contact Us Page

Your Contact Us page is vital for potential clients to reach out to you. It should be user-friendly, accessible, and inviting. Key components include:

1. **Clear contact information.** Provide multiple contact options such as email, phone number, and physical address (if applicable).

2. **Contact form.** Include a simple, straightforward contact form. Ask only essential information to avoid overwhelming visitors.

3. **Social media links.** Add links to your social media profiles, offering additional ways to connect.

4. **Response time.** Set expectations by mentioning the typical response time.

5. **Map and directions.** If you have a physical location, include a map and directions.

6. **FAQ sections.** Consider adding a Frequently Asked Questions (FAQ) section to address common inquiries.

Your Contact Us page should encourage communication, foster trust, and provide a hassle-free way for visitors to get in touch with you.

Example: NoahStJohn.com/connect.

Your Sales Funnels: The Spokes

If your website is the hub, your sales funnels are the spokes. Most of your organic traffic will go to your website, but your paid traffic will generally go to your spokes. (I'll discuss these in detail in chapter 5, on 7-Figure Client Attraction Secrets.)

Entire books have been written on sales funnels, so there's a lot we could cover on this topic. However, almost everyone who I've coached over the last ten years has heard a lot about sales funnels—yet most still haven't built their own yet.

That's why a big part of my job as a mentor is to help people get out of their own way so they can start to make big money online. That being the case, let me simplify the process of sales funnels so you can launch your first (or next) funnel faster and easier.

My team and I have built over 200 sales funnels for myself and my clients over the last seven years. That's more funnel pages than most people will ever build in their lifetimes.

The great news for you is that you only need to focus on four funnel pages in order to make good money online. I call these the Four Fundamental Funnel Pages. (Yes, I'm putting the *fun* back in *funnel*!)

The Four Fundamental Funnel Pages are:

1. **Landing page.** Where you send traffic.
2. **One-Time Offer page.** Where you offer an upsell.
3. **Confirmation page.** Where you confirm your customer's purchase.
4. **Membership page.** Where you deliver your product that your customer bought.

"That's it, Noah?"

Yep, that's it!

Now let me walk you through each one of these Fundamental Pages in turn.

Fundamental Funnel Page 1: Landing Page

Also known as a sales/order page, this is the page where you're going to send traffic and take orders. It's also where customers make the decision to purchase your product or service. This is why you need to spend a great deal of time and attention to make sure this page converts as many visitors to buyers as possible.

Essential elements for a high-converting sales/order page include:

1. **Compelling headlines.** Engage visitors immediately with clear, benefit-driven headlines.
2. **Product description.** Detailed yet concise descriptions outlining the benefits and features.

3. **High-quality images and videos.** Visual representations of the product or service to enhance understanding and trust.

4. **Testimonials and reviews.** Social proof to build credibility and reassure potential buyers.

5. **Clear pricing.** Transparent pricing structures with different options or packages, if applicable.

6. **Strong call to action (CTA).** Direct and clear CTA buttons or links for making the purchase.

7. **Guarantees and refund policies.** Include money-back guarantees or refund policies to alleviate purchase risks.

8. **FAQ section.** Address common queries and concerns to facilitate the decision-making process.

The goal is to guide visitors through the buying process smoothly, providing all the necessary information and reassurance they need to complete the purchase.

Fundamental Funnel Page 2: One-Time Offer (OTO) Page

A One-Time Offer (OTO) page is designed to create urgency and encourage immediate action by offering a special deal, typically seen after a customer has made an initial purchase or commitment. To effectively convert visitors, it should include:

1. **Exclusive offer.** Clearly state the uniqueness and limited availability of the offer.

2. **Value proposition.** Emphasize the benefits and how they complement the initial purchase.

3. **Urgency and scarcity.** Use countdown timers or limited quantity indicators to prompt quick decision-making.

4. **Clear call to action.** Ensure that the CTA stands out and directly relates to the offer.

5. **Risk reversal.** Include guarantees or easy cancellation options to reduce perceived risk.

6. **Testimonials or endorsements.** Provide credibility through customer reviews or expert endorsements.

The key is to present the OTO as a valuable, time-sensitive opportunity that enhances the customer's initial purchase, focusing on how it offers speed or automation benefits. Note that you can have anywhere from one to three unique OTOs per funnel, as long as the offers align with the original product.

Fundamental Funnel Page 3: Confirmation Page

A confirmation page is crucial in finalizing a customer's online purchase. It reassures the customer that their transaction was successful. Key elements include:

1. **Clear confirmation message.** A straightforward "thank-you" or "order confirmed" message.

2. **Order details.** Summarize the purchase, including details of product or service, price, and quantity.

3. **Transaction number.** Provide an order or transaction number for reference.

4. **Next steps.** Inform the customer about shipping, delivery timelines, and how to access or track their purchase.

5. **Customer support contact.** Offer contact information for customer service in case of queries or issues.

6. **Cross-selling opportunities.** Suggest related products or services.

7. **Social proof or testimonials.** Reinforce the purchase decision with positive feedback from other customers.

This page is not just a receipt but an opportunity to build trust, encourage future interactions, and increase customer satisfaction.

Fundamental Funnel Page 4: Membership Area

A membership area is a dedicated space for delivering your online courses, products, or events. Key elements for an effective membership area include:

1. **User-friendly interface.** A clear and intuitive layout allowing easy navigation through content.

2. **Personalized welcome.** A customized greeting or introduction for new members.

3. **Content organization.** Well-structured modules or sections for easy access to courses or materials.

4. **Progress tracking.** Features that allow users to track their progress through courses or content.

5. **Community features.** Forums or discussion boards to foster community and interaction among members.

6. **Support resources.** Access to help or support, like FAQs, contact forms, or live chat.

7. **Regular updates.** Continuous addition of new content or updates to existing materials to keep the membership valuable.

This area should offer a seamless and engaging experience, enhancing the value of your offering and encouraging long-term membership retention.

Now It's Decision Time

Now that I've laid all this out for you, it's decision time: you must decide how you're going to get your website built and who is going to do it. One reason so many "wantrepreneurs" never make money online (or stay stuck at the income level they're at) is because they put off making important decisions, waiting for everything to be perfect.

Yet you and I both know that nothing is ever perfect and you can never see the full outcome of your decisions ahead of time. Therefore, when deciding whether to build your online funnel yourself or have it done for you, consider the following options. While there are dozens of different platforms to build your website and funnels on, I personally use and recommend to my clients to use the following resources:

Do It Yourself (DIY) Option

Clickfunnels offers a platform to build your funnels with ease. Get a free 14-day trial at **ClickNoah.com.**

Done for You Options

Dr. Noah's Done for You Website Design & Social Media Management. My team specializes in building your online hub website using the Foundational 5 Formula, saving you the hassle of doing it yourself. Visit **NoahStJohn.com/design** for this service.

Dr. Noah's Done for You Inner Circle. For a complete funnel creation, my team and I will handle everything for you.

Learn more at **NoahStJohn.com/doneforyou**.

Evaluate your time, money, and effort budget to decide which route is most feasible for you. DIY options offer more control and hands-on experience, whereas Done for You services provide professional expertise, which will save you time and money in the long run. Choose wisely to align with your business goals and resources.

THIS IS THE DIFFERENCE BETWEEN DIY AND DONE FOR YOU.

Choosing Payment Processor and Email Platform

Choosing the right payment processor and email platform is crucial for your online business, because the wrong choice can cost you thousands of dollars and countless hours wasted. For example, the wrong choice of a payment processor for your online business can result in significant financial losses. If you opt for a payment processor with high transaction fees or hidden charges, your profit margins can be significantly impacted. Additionally, if the chosen payment processor lacks robust security measures, your business may become vulnerable to fraudulent transactions or data breaches, leading to financial liabilities and reputational damage.

Similarly, selecting the wrong email platform for your online business can lead to wasted time and financial losses. An inadequate email platform may place limitations on the number of subscribers or emails you can send, forcing you to upgrade to a more expensive plan. Moreover, if the platform lacks reliable deliverability rates or advanced automation features, your marketing campaigns may not reach your intended audience effectively, resulting in missed opportunities for sales and customer engagement.

By making the right choices in these areas, you can save costs, maximize revenue, and allocate your resources efficiently, ultimately contributing to the success and growth of your online business.

Here are the ones I personally use and recommend to my coaching clients:

ClickNoah.com (a **Clickfunnels** label). Easy-to-use platform for building sales funnels and email list management. Visit ClickNoah.com.

Stripe. A versatile online payment processor. Sign up for free at Stripe.com.

PayPal. A widely recognized online payment system. Sign up for free at PayPal.com.

Build, Launch, Test

Now we come to the part where the rubber meets the road: building, launching, and testing your online cash machine. Wantrepreneurs will keep all of this knowledge in their heads and never move forward, out of fear. Entrepreneurs, on the other hand, realize that failure is simply feedback, and that if something is worth doing, it's worth doing really badly at first, then getting better over time. Therefore, I encourage you to follow these steps:

1. Build Your Sales Funnel

Utilize one of the previously mentioned methods to construct your sales funnel. This step involves integrating your chosen payment processors and crafting the funnel flow, including landing pages, sales pages, and thank-you pages.

2. Initial Testing with Friends and Contacts

Invite your friends and social media contacts to go through your funnel. Ask specifically if they encounter any issues or if any part of the funnel seems unclear or complicated.

3. Iterative Improvement

If feedback indicates any sticking points, refine and test repeatedly. This is a crucial phase where tweaking and optimizing your funnel ensures a smooth customer journey. It's better to identify and resolve issues now rather than after a full launch, when you're spending money to drive traffic.

4. Launch and Drive Traffic

Once your funnel is polished and ready, launch it to a broader audience. Use the traffic strategies outlined in chapter 5 to attract visitors to your funnel. This might include SEO, social media marketing, email campaigns, paid advertising, or a combination thereof.

Jane's Story

Jane was a dedicated fitness coach with a deep passion for helping others. However, her digital presence was minimal, her website barely attracted any visitors, and her online income was nonexistent. Frustrated and seeking a change, she discovered my 12-Week Breakthrough coaching program.

Joining my program marked the beginning of Jane's transformation, because we provide not just strategies, but a holistic approach to building a successful online business. Jane absorbed every lesson, eager to implement these newfound strategies.

Guided by my teachings, Jane started by overhauling her website. It wasn't just about aesthetics; it was about creating a platform that clearly communicated her unique value and invited visitors to engage with her services. She infused her site with her personality and passion, making it a true representation of her brand.

Jane's journey through the 12-Week Breakthrough was a blend of learning and action. In just six months, her online presence went from nearly zero to a buzzing hub of activity. Her revamped website is now a lead-generating machine.

In addition, Jane's income saw a remarkable turnaround. From struggling to make ends meet, she began generating a consistent six-figure income. Her online business was no longer just a dream; it's now a thriving reality, thanks to the actionable steps and unwavering support she received from the 12-Week Breakthrough program.

Jane's story is more than just a success story; it's a journey of empowerment. By following my teachings, she not only transformed her business but also her life, proving that with the right guidance and an open heart, remarkable change is indeed possible.

The Longer You Wait, The Greater the Weight

In the journey of constructing your cash machine website and sales funnels, there lies a crucial principle: *the longer you wait, the greater the weight*. This statement encapsulates the burden of procrastination and its compounding effect on your entrepreneurial aspirations.

The more you delay the creation of your cash machine website and sales funnels, the heavier the burden of unfinished business becomes. Procrastination isn't just about delayed action; it's a cumulative weight that grows over time, making the task seem more daunting than it actually is. This growing weight can lead to increased anxiety and doubt, often resulting in a paralyzing effect that hinders progress.

Time is a nonrenewable resource, and every moment you're not present online is a missed opportunity. Delaying your entry or expansion online means missing out on potential clients, sales, and crucial market insights. As you wait, your competitors are moving forward, capturing the audience that could have been yours.

THE LONGER YOU WAIT, THE GREATER THE WEIGHT.

The longer you wait, the more you have to catch up. This compounding effect means that the effort required to start later will be significantly more than if you had begun earlier. In the digital age, playing catch-up is much harder than leading the pack from the outset.

To overcome the inertia of procrastination, start with small, manageable steps. Break down the process of building your website and sales funnels into smaller tasks, and tackle them one at a time.

Imperfect action is better than perfect inaction. Launching a basic version of your website or a simple funnel is infinitely more valuable than waiting to create the "perfect" version. You can always refine and improve as you go. The key is to start and gain momentum.

As you work on building your cash machine website and sales funnels, embrace speed and immediacy. Let go of the need for perfection and focus on progress. In the world of online business, action breeds success, and the sooner you start, the lighter the journey will be.

In our next chapter, I'll give you my 7-Figure List Building Secrets, which have enabled me and my clients to rapidly increase sales and revenues using the power of email marketing. See you there!

4

My 7-Figure List Building Secrets

It's much cheaper, faster, and easier to sell something to someone who knows, likes, and trusts you than to someone who doesn't.

—NOAH ST. JOHN

Email marketing has been a pivotal component of Internet marketing since the 1990s. It began as a simple method for brands to communicate with their audience but has evolved into a sophisticated tool for targeted, personalized messaging. Early email campaigns were broad and often unsophisticated, leading to the advent of spam.

As technology advanced, so did the strategies for email marketing. Today it remains a workhorse in the digital marketing world because of its direct and personal reach to customers. Unlike other marketing channels, emails land in a user's personal inbox, making it a more intimate form of communication. The evolution of data analytics and segmentation tools has further enhanced email marketing, allowing businesses to send highly targeted messages based on user behavior, preferences, and demographics.

Moreover, email marketing boasts a significant return on investment (ROI). For every dollar spent on email marketing, businesses can expect an average return of $42, making it one of the most effective forms of online marketing. It's a critical tool for businesses to build relationships, nurture leads, and drive conversions, making it indispensable in a comprehensive digital marketing strategy.

In the 1990s, when email was a novelty, open rates (that is, the rate at which emails are actually opened by recipients) were exceptionally high, often exceeding 90 percent. Because the medium was so new, people were more eager to open and read every email they received. As email became ubiquitous, open rates gradually declined. Today, average open rates are significantly lower, often around 20–25 percent. This decrease can be attributed to several factors, including the sheer volume of emails people receive daily, the rise of spam, and the development of more sophisticated email filtering by service providers.

Despite these challenges, email marketing remains a cornerstone of online marketing campaigns. Its effectiveness lies in its ability to directly deliver targeted, personalized content, fostering a more personal connection with customers. Email also allows for consistent engagement with and nurturing of leads, playing a crucial role in converting prospects into customers. Its direct nature, combined with the ability to track and analyze user engagement, makes it invaluable for understanding and responding to customer behavior and preferences.

When I launched SuccessClinic.com in 1997, email marketing was one of the only forms of marketing that was affordable enough for me to use, because I was operating on a shoestring budget. At the beginning, my open rates averaged 70–90 percent. Of course, those days are long gone—yet I still have people who have been on my email list since the 1990s!

Having subscribers who have stayed on my email list that long since the 1990s is a testament to the value and relevance of the content I provide. Several key factors keep these long-term subscribers engaged:

1. **Consistent value.** My emails consistently offer valuable insights, tips, and solutions that resonate with my audience's needs and interests. This consistent delivery of value keeps them engaged and interested in what I have to say.

2. **Personal connection.** Over the years, I've built a personal connection with my audience. My emails often include personal stories, experiences, and ongoing learning, making my content relatable and authentic.

3. **Content evolution.** As my audience's needs and interests have evolved, so has the content of my emails. This adaptability ensures that my emails remain relevant and beneficial to my subscribers.

4. **Interactivity and responsiveness.** I encourage feedback and actively engage with my subscribers. This two-way communication makes my audience feel heard and valued, fostering a sense of community and loyalty.

5. **Quality over quantity.** I focus on the quality of content rather than bombarding my subscribers with frequent but less meaningful emails. This approach respects their time and attention, making each email they receive from me worthwhile.

These factors help explain why people stay on my list for decades, reflecting a strong, mutually beneficial relationship between me and my subscribers.

How to Build Your Email List from Scratch

When I tell my clients about my startup experiences, they frequently respond, "That's great for you, Noah—but I didn't launch my online business in the nineties. How do I start my email list if I don't have one yet?"

If I were just starting out today and didn't have the benefit of more than two decades of experience, here's exactly what I would do:

1. **Choose an email marketing platform.** Select a reliable email marketing service like ClickNoah. com, Constant Contact, or AWeber. These platforms offer tools to create, send, and track emails.

2. **Create a lead magnet.** Offer something valuable for free in exchange for an email address. This could be an ebook, a webinar, a discount code, or an exclusive video.

3. **Create a sign-up form.** Integrate a sign-up form on your website. Place it prominently on your home page, blog, and other key pages. Make it enticing and simple for visitors to subscribe.

4. **Email campaigns.** Once you have subscribers, engage them with regular, value-packed emails. Avoid spammy content, and focus on providing useful information. I will provide specific examples below in my Campaign Profit Blueprint.

5. **Track and optimize.** Monitor the performance of your emails and sign-up forms. Use analytics to understand what works, and continuously optimize your strategy.

6. **Offer exclusive deals or insider access.** Give your subscribers something they can't get anywhere else. This encourages sign-ups and increases perceived value.

My Campaign Profit Blueprint

Because email marketing is the cornerstone of all online marketing, I created my **Campaign Profit Blueprint.** This is an integrated sequence of email campaigns that I have written and entered into my email marketing platform (in my case, ClickNoah.com).

My Campaign Profit Blueprint is a strategic approach to email marketing designed to enhance and scale up marketing results. It's an integrated sequence of email campaigns that are meticulously written and implemented into an email marketing platform.

The blueprint's significance lies in its structured and systematic nature, ensuring consistent communication with the email list. It encompasses a variety of campaigns, each tailored to different stages of the customer journey, from initial engagement to conversion.

By having this structured sequence in place, you can systematically nurture leads, build relationships, and ultimately increase conversions more effectively. This methodical approach is crucial for scaling up email marketing efforts, as it aligns marketing messages with the audience's needs and interests at each step, leading to higher engagement and profitability.

Let's look at each phase of my Campaign Profit Blueprint.

Phase 1: Welcome

The Welcome phase in my Campaign Profit Blueprint is pivotal for setting the tone of your relationship with new subscribers. It's focused on ensuring people engage with your *lead magnet*: the free resource offered in exchange for providing their email address. This phase usually comprises a series of emails that greet new subscribers warmly and guide them towards utilizing the lead magnet.

These emails are crucial because they initiate the subscriber's journey with your brand. A well-crafted Welcome email should express gratitude for the subscription, clearly restate the value of the lead magnet, and provide easy access to it. It's about making a positive first impression, reinforcing the subscriber's decision to join your list, and beginning to build trust.

Furthermore, the Welcome emails are an opportunity to set expectations. You can outline the type of content that subscribers should anticipate, how often they'll receive emails, and encourage them to whitelist your email address to ensure they receive all communications. This phase is not just about delivering the lead magnet; it's about starting a conversation, fostering engagement, and laying the groundwork for a long-term relationship.

Phase 2: Ascension

Phase 2 of my Campaign Profit Blueprint, the Ascension phase, is where you elevate the relationship with your subscribers by promoting your product. This phase kicks in after a subscriber has engaged with your lead magnet.

The key focus here is to guide subscribers from consuming free content to considering a purchase.

The Ascension emails should seamlessly connect the value obtained from the lead magnet to the enhanced benefits of your paid offerings. These emails are crafted to showcase how your products or services are a natural next step for those who found value in your lead magnet. These emails need to be persuasive yet not pushy, highlighting the advantages of your product in a way that resonates with the needs and interests of your audience.

Use testimonials, success stories, or case studies to reinforce the value of your offerings. The Ascension phase is crucial for transitioning a casual subscriber into a potential customer, so it's important to ensure that your messaging is clear, compelling, and directly tied to the interests that led them to subscribe initially.

Phase 3: Everlaunch

Phase 3 of my Campaign Profit Blueprint, Everlaunch, is short for *evergreen launch*. This phase revolves around an evergreen launch strategy, where your products or services are continuously promoted to new subscribers in a systematic, ongoing manner. The idea is to create a perpetual cycle of engagement and sales opportunities.

In the Everlaunch phase, emails are carefully crafted to mimic a live product launch, providing an immersive experience for each new subscriber as if they are participating in a real-time event. The key here is to maintain the excitement and urgency of a traditional product launch, but in a way that is automated and consistently refreshed for new audience members. These emails should include:

1. **An introduction to your offer.** Introduce your product or service in a way that resonates with the needs and interests of the subscriber, piqued by the lead magnet phase.

2. **Testimonials and social proof.** Share success stories and testimonials to build credibility and trust.

3. **Value-added content.** Provide valuable information or insights related to your offer, which underscores why it matters and its usefulness.

4. **Urgency and call to action.** Create a sense of urgency (limited time offers, exclusive bonuses) to encourage prompt action.

5. **Consistent follow-ups.** Follow up regularly with additional information, answers to common questions, and reminders of the offer's benefits and deadline.

This phase is crucial because it keeps your offer front and center in the minds of your subscribers, capitalizing on the initial interest sparked by your lead magnet. By effectively implementing the Everlaunch phase, you can significantly increase your sales while nurturing a long-term relationship with your audience.

Phase 4: Everclass

Phase 4 of my Campaign Profit Blueprint, Everclass, is short for *evergreen web class*. This phase focuses on leveraging webinars to both educate your audience and promote your products. It is essential for nurturing trust and demonstrating the real-world application and benefits of your offerings. These emails should include:

1. **Educational webinar content.** Design a webinar that provides genuine value, teaching your audience something beneficial while naturally leading into the promotion of your product.

2. **Seamless transition to offer.** Ensure a smooth transition from the educational portion to the product pitch. This should feel like a natural progression rather than a hard sell.

3. **Clear call to action.** End the webinar with a strong, clear call to action that guides attendees on what to do next if they're interested in your product.

4. **Follow-up emails.** After the webinar, send follow-up emails to attendees. Include a summary of the webinar, additional resources, and a reminder of the product offer.

5. **Evergreen setup.** The Everclass should be set up in an Evergreen format, allowing new subscribers to access the webinar as if it were happening live, creating a continuous cycle of engagement and sales opportunities.

This phase will help you establish your expertise, build rapport, and guide potential customers from being interested learners to committed buyers. By effectively executing the Everclass phase, you can create a powerful tool for ongoing lead generation and sales conversion.

Phase 5: Trust Builder

Phase 5 of my Campaign Profit Blueprint, Trust Builder, is designed to deepen the relationship with your audience by offering them value and occasionally promoting your products. This phase is vital for maintaining engagement and fostering long-term customer loyalty. These emails should include:

1. **Value-added content.** Regularly deliver content that is informative, helpful, and relevant to your

audience's interests and needs. This could be in the form of articles, tips, industry insights, or personal anecdotes that resonate with your audience.

2. **Subtle product promotion.** Integrate gentle promotions of your products or services into your content. This should not be the primary focus but rather a soft recommendation or a natural extension of the value you're providing.

3. **Consistency and frequency.** Establish a regular schedule for sending out your emails. Consistency helps in keeping your audience engaged and looking forward to your content.

By effectively executing the Trust Builder phase, you not only maintain a continual line of communication with your audience but also position yourself as a trusted authority, which can lead to increased sales over time.

Phase 6: Flash Sale

Phase 6 of my Campaign Profit Blueprint is Flash Sale, a strategic phase where you offer a limited-time sale on one of your products. This phase is critical for creating urgency and boosting sales. This phase should include:

1. **Limited-time offer.** Announce a sale on a specific product, clearly stating the time limit. This creates a sense of urgency, encouraging quick action from your audience.

2. **Attractive discounts.** Provide a significant discount or added value to make the offer irresistible. Ensure that the discount is substantial enough to motivate immediate purchases.

3. **Targeted communication.** Use email to target prospects who have shown interest in your products but haven't bought yet. Tailor your messaging to highlight the benefits of the offer and the urgency of the time-limited deal.

4. **Clear call to action.** Each email should have a clear and compelling call to action (CTA) that directs the recipient to the sales page where they can make the purchase.

The Flash Sale phase is a powerful tool for driving sales and clearing inventory, but it's important to use it sparingly to avoid diluting its effectiveness.

Phase 7: Affiliate Getting

Phase 7 of my Campaign Profit Blueprint is Affiliate Getting, which focuses on leveraging affiliates to promote your products or services. This phase is essential for expanding your reach and tapping into new audiences through partnerships. Key components include:

1. **Recruitment of affiliates.** Identify and reach out to potential affiliates who align with your brand and have access to your target audience. Utilize your networks, industry contacts, and social media to find suitable partners.

2. **Clear communication.** Clearly convey the benefits of partnering with you, including commission structures, promotional materials, and support provided. Transparency builds trust and encourages affiliates to actively promote your offerings.

3. **Inclusion of marketing tools.** Supply your affiliates with effective marketing materials, such as email templates, banners, and social media posts. These resources should align with your brand voice and message for consistency.

4. **Regular updates and motivation.** Keep your affiliates engaged with regular updates about product developments, sales strategies, and success stories. Motivate them with incentives, contests, or recognition for top performers.

5. **Performance tracking.** Implement systems to track affiliate performance, sales generated,

and commissions owed. This ensures fair compensation and identifies high-performing affiliates for future collaborations.

The Affiliate Getting phase can help you to build a reliable network of partners who can extend your reach and contribute significantly to your sales.

How to Get Fill-in-the-Blank Templates
(So You Don't Have to Start from Scratch)

If you want to follow specific examples of each phase of my Campaign Profit Blueprint, I created them for you in my online course called 7-Figure Machine (cool name, huh?).

Did you ever play Mad Libs when you were a kid? Mad Libs is a word game created back in the fifties, in which you fill in the blanks on a page marked with directions for adding parts of speech—"adjective" or "noun"—to create a funny message or story.

In the 7-Figure Machine online course, I've created something that will save you tons of time and money: marketing Mad Libs. My version consists of fully customizable email templates, where you simply fill in the blanks with your product or service details. This means you don't have to start from scratch but can launch your Campaign Profit Blueprint armed with proven money-making templates. In fact, developing these templates cost me over $250,000; however, you can have them for pennies on the dollar. (You're welcome!)

This course not only provides detailed, step-by-step examples and strategies to implement each phase effectively; it's also designed to help you build a robust email marketing campaign, from the Welcome phase to the Affiliate Getting phase, ensuring that every step contributes to your success. Discover the full potential of email marketing and learn how to turn your email list into a profitable asset by enrolling at **7FigureMachine.com.**

Build, Launch, Test

Just as we need to build, launch, and test your website and sales funnels, you need to do the same with your email marketing, or Campaign Profit Blueprint. Here's where to start:

1. Decide if you're going to do it yourself or hire someone else to do it for you.

2. Create your campaigns. Just as you did with building your sales funnel, start by creating your email campaigns using my Campaign Profit Blueprint or a similar method. This step includes integrating your email platform and crafting

a sequence that aligns with your marketing strategy.

3. Feedback and initial testing: a process similar to testing your funnel. Invite friends and social media contacts to engage with your email campaign. Seek feedback on any unclear or complicated elements. This early feedback is vital to ensure the effectiveness of your campaign.

4. Refinement and improvement. As with your funnel, use the feedback to refine your email campaigns. It's a continuous process of testing, getting feedback, and improving. This approach ensures that by the time you're ready for a wider launch, your campaign is polished and more likely to succeed.

Michael's Story

Michael, a talented life coach specializing in career transitions, faced a common hurdle: his email list was virtually nonexistent. Despite having insightful content and valuable services, he struggled to reach his audience online. This all changed when he enrolled in my 12-Week Breakthrough coaching program.

Michael decided to join my program because he understood the need to harness the power of email marketing. The 12-Week Breakthrough provided him with the tools and knowledge necessary to build a robust email list from scratch.

Michael began by crafting an irresistible lead magnet. He developed a free ebook which addressed the immediate needs of his target audience. I also showed him how to optimize his website for more efficient lead capture.

Following my advice, Michael regularly sent out informative and engaging emails. These emails were not just promotional but provided real value, establishing trust and credibility with his audience.

Within just a few months, Michael's email list grew exponentially. His open rates and engagement levels surged, indicating a growing interest in his content and services. The email list became his primary source of new client inquiries and bookings.

From having a nonexistent email list, Michael transitioned to having a thriving community of engaged subscribers. His online visibility and business growth were no longer stagnant but dynamically increasing.

He attributed this success to the comprehensive strategies and continuous support he received from the 12-Week Breakthrough coaching program. Michael's journey highlights the potential of well-executed email strategies in building a sustainable and profitable online business.

The More You Delay, The More You'll Pay

The fact is, every day that you don't execute the strategies I'm teaching you in this book equates to lost revenue and lost opportunity. In the fast-paced digital world, time is directly linked to money. Delay in launching any part of your 7-Figure Machine means missed sales, unengaged audiences, and a slower journey to profitability. Your online presence is an investment, and like with all investments, the sooner you begin, the sooner you reap the rewards.

Beyond direct financial loss, delaying incurs significant opportunity costs. These are the benefits you miss out on by choosing inaction over action. This includes not just potential income but also the lost chance for brand exposure, network expansion, and customer feedback that could refine your offerings. In a constantly evolving market, being late can mean missing the wave entirely.

The digital market doesn't pause. As you delay, your competitors advance, adopting new technologies and strategies that capture your share of the market. When you eventually do enter the fray, you're not just starting from where you were; you're starting from behind. The cost of catching up can often exceed the initial investment required to launch on time.

Delay often breeds more delay. This psychological cost manifests as dwindling confidence, increased fear of failure, and a skewed perception of the task at hand. The longer you wait, the harder it becomes to start, creating a self-perpetuating cycle of procrastination that becomes increasingly costly to break.

THE MORE YOU DELAY, THE MORE YOU'LL PAY.

To mitigate these costs, focus on implementing these instructions with clear deadlines. Break each project into smaller, manageable tasks and set realistic timelines for each.

The digital marketplace is unforgiving to those who wait too long. Recognize that the perfect time rarely comes, and the best time is often now. The immediacy with which you act can set the tone for your business's trajectory. Quick, decisive action is rewarded with early insights, adaptable strategies, and a robust foundation for scaling.

The path to success is paved with timely actions and the willingness to dive in, even when the waters seem uncertain. In the dynamic world of online business, now is always the best time to start.

In our next chapter, I'll share my 7-Figure Client Attraction Secrets that have enabled me and my clients to reach a global audience through the power of online traffic strategies without breaking the bank. Let's go!

5

My 7-Figure Client Attraction Secrets

Effective marketing means you're
able to serve more people in a world
that desperately needs your help.
—NOAH ST. JOHN

To have a successful online business, you're going to need to attract customers and clients. Historically, the evolution of marketing strategies has always centered around attracting and retaining clients. In the pre-Internet era, businesses relied on traditional advertising methods like print, radio, and television, but these lacked the precision and personalization capabilities of today's digital marketing. The advent of the Internet and social media revolutionized client attraction, enabling businesses to target specific demographics with personalized content.

The Why It Matters of client attraction in the digital age cannot be overstated. Effective client attraction strategies, like the ones I'll present in this chapter, convert prospects into loyal customers and clients, fostering growth and profitability. These strategies offer the advantage of reaching a global audience at a relatively low cost compared to that of traditional marketing methods.

Client attraction is not just about reaching a wide audience; it's about reaching the *right* audience. It involves understanding your ideal client's needs, behaviors, and preferences. By tailoring content and offers to meet these needs, you can create a strong connection with your potential clients.

In today's competitive digital landscape, mastering client attraction is essential for any business aspiring to reach seven-figure revenue. It's not just about selling a product or service; it's about creating value, building relationships, and establishing trust. Businesses that excel in attracting and retaining clients are those that understand and adapt to the ever-changing online marketplace, always staying ahead of the curve in meeting their clients' evolving needs.

The Difference Between Customers and Clients

The terms *customers* and *clients* are often used interchangeably, but to me, they signify different business relationships.

Customers are typically those who purchase products or services in a transactional manner, often with a focus on the exchange itself. They might engage in one-time or occasional purchases, yet their interaction with the business is usually limited to the buying process.

The term *client*, on the other hand, implies a longer-term, more relational interaction, often associated with services, particularly in professional sectors like legal, consulting, or coaching. Relationships with clients are more personalized and involve a deeper understanding of their needs, preferences, and goals.

Businesses serving clients usually focus on providing tailored solutions, advice, and ongoing support, emphasizing a partnership or advisory role rather than just a transactional one.

This distinction highlights the different approaches businesses might take in their marketing and service strategies, depending on whether they are targeting customers or clients.

Focusing on customers, who engage in transactional purchases, often leads to quicker sales but might not foster long-term loyalty. The benefit here is the potential for a broad customer base and high volume of sales. The downside is the lack of deep relationships, which can result in lower customer retention rates.

Concentrating on clients, who require more personalized services, builds stronger, long-term relationships. This often translates to higher trust and potentially higher-value contracts. The drawback is the need for more time and resources to maintain these relationships, and potentially fewer overall transactions compared to a customer-focused approach.

In fact, both strategies have their distinct advantages and challenges, and that's why at SuccessClinic.com, we serve both customers and clients.

My MAPSSS Method for Client Attraction

My MAPSSS Method for Client Attraction encapsulates a comprehensive approach to client attraction, covering all of the main ways to maximize your online marketing reach and impact. This allows for a highly diversified strategy, tapping into different markets and preferences.

By utilizing every phase of my MAPSSS Method, you'll not only spread your message across multiple platforms, you'll also reach your potential clients at various touchpoints. This diversification ensures that you're not reliant on a single source for client acquisition, making your business more resilient and adaptable to changing market dynamics.

Each phase of my MAPSSS Method targets a specific aspect of client attraction, creating a well-rounded and effective strategy. *MAPSSS* stands for:

- Media
- Affiliate marketing
- Pay-per-click advertising
- Speaking
- SEO (Search Engine Optimization)
- Social media marketing

Let's examine each phase of my MAPSSS Method in turn.

Phase 1: Media

In this digital age, media outlets have a broader spectrum than ever. Understanding the types of media you can leverage is essential for visibility and brand building. Your target media outlets should include:

1. **TV (local and national).** Television, both local and national, remains a powerful medium. It offers broad reach and can significantly increase your visibility.

2. **Radio (local and national).** Radio, like TV, spans local and national audiences. It's especially useful for reaching people during commutes.

3. **Podcasts.** The rise of podcasts has been meteoric. They offer a more engaged niche audience, often looking for in-depth information.

4. **Newspapers and magazines.** Print media, while declining, still holds clout, especially for a more mature audience.

5. **Your own newsletter** to your email list. Many business owners forget that their own email list is a form of media that should be leveraged consistently. Regular newsletters keep your audience engaged and informed.

ACTION STEPS TO UTILIZE MEDIA EFFECTIVELY

1. **Craft a compelling pitch.** Your pitch to media outlets should be concise, intriguing, and tailored to the specific audience of the outlet. It should highlight why your story or expertise is relevant and valuable to their viewers or readers.

2. **Reach out to producers and media outlets.** Identify the right contacts (such as producers and editors) and send your pitch directly to them. Personalize your emails for a better response rate.

3. **Participate in interviews.** Once you secure an opportunity, ensure that you're well-prepared for the interview. Provide insightful and valuable content that resonates with the audience.

4. **Deliver value during the interview.** Focus on giving actionable advice or unique perspectives during your media appearances. Avoid overt selling and instead concentrate on establishing yourself as a thought leader in your field.

5. **Direct the audience for further engagement.** At the end of your media appearance, guide the audience to where they can find more information about your work. This could be your website, social media channels, or a specific landing page.

KEY CONSIDERATIONS

1. **Media training.** Consider getting media training to enhance your communication skills, especially for TV and radio appearances.

2. **Follow-up.** After your appearance, follow up with the outlet and thank them. This can help build a relationship for future opportunities.

3. **Leverage appearances.** Use your media appearances in your marketing materials and on social media to boost credibility and reach.

By following these steps and strategically targeting various media outlets, you can significantly increase your visibility, establish credibility, and attract more clients to your business.

Example: See **MeetNoah.com** for how I consistently leverage media appearances to attract clients.

Phase 2: Affiliate Marketing

Affiliate marketing is a type of business relationship whereby you reward individuals (affiliates) for each customer they bring to your business through their marketing efforts. It can be a powerful tool in your digital marketing toolbox, because it leverages the networks and efforts of others to drive sales for your products or services.

KEY COMPONENTS OF AFFILIATE MARKETING

1. **Commission-based system.** The cornerstone of affiliate marketing is the commission-based reward system. Affiliates earn a portion of the sale for every customer they refer to you.

2. **Custom links.** You must provide each affiliate with unique links that track the sales they generate. This ensures accurate tracking and fair compensation.

3. **Mutually beneficial relationship.** It's a win-win-win scenario: you gain increased sales and wider visibility, affiliates earn through their promotional efforts, and your customers and clients win because they get to experience your transformational products and services.

ACTION STEPS FOR EFFECTIVE AFFILIATE MARKETING

1. **Set up your affiliate program.** Utilize platforms like **ClickNoah.com** to create your products and set up an affiliate program. Ensure that your system accurately tracks sales and commissions.

2. **Recruit affiliates.** Start by inviting friends, business associates, or industry influencers to join your affiliate program. Look for individuals who have a strong presence in your target market and can authentically promote your products.

3. **Provide resources to affiliates.** Equip your affiliates with the necessary tools to succeed, such as custom links, promotional materials, and insights into your target audience. Clear communication regarding your products and

ideal customers can significantly enhance their marketing efforts.

4. **Track and reward sales.** Monitor the sales generated through each affiliate link. Ensure timely and accurate payments to maintain a healthy relationship with your affiliates.

5. **Continuous engagement.** Regularly engage with your affiliates, providing them with updates on new products, promotional strategies, and feedback on their performance. Encouraging and supporting your affiliates can lead to more effective promotions and increased sales.

6. **Promote with purpose.** As an affiliate, focus on promoting products that align with your audience's interests and needs. Authenticity in promotion leads to higher conversion rates.

7. **Observe and learn.** Pay attention to the strategies and communication used in successful affiliate programs. Apply these learnings to enhance your own affiliate marketing efforts.

Affiliate marketing, when executed well, can exponentially increase your reach and sales, making it an essential component of your client attraction strategy.

To experience this process firsthand, join our Affiliate Program. By participating in an established affiliate program like ours, you can gain practical insights into how affiliate marketing works. This hands-on experience can be invaluable in understanding the nuances of managing an effective affiliate program. Join for free at **NoahStJohn.com/jv.**

Phase 3: Pay-per-Click Advertising

Pay-per-click (PPC) marketing is a dynamic aspect of online advertising where you pay a fee each time someone clicks on your ads. It's the most direct way to buy visits to your website or sales funnel, as opposed to earning those visits organically. The Big Three platforms for PPC are YouTube, Google, and Facebook/Instagram (which has been rebranded as Meta), each offering unique advantages for targeting and reach.

Since every advertising platform is unique, attempting an in-depth analysis of each one is beyond the scope of this book. In addition, new platforms continually spring up, each offering a unique set of targeted potential buyers. Here's a brief overview of how PPC advertising works, along with its pros and cons.

This overview provides a foundational understanding essential for anyone considering leveraging PPC as part of their client attraction strategy. The key to success in PPC is not just in launching ads, but in continuously monitoring, analyzing, and refining them to ensure they efficiently meet your business objectives.

THE MECHANICS OF PPC

1. **Platform selection.** Choose from the Big Three (YouTube, Google, Meta) based on where your target audience is most active and the nature of your product or service.

2. **Cost model.** You pay the chosen platform for each click your ad receives. This model allows for precise budgeting and tracking of return on investment (ROI).

3. **Ad creation and optimization.** Develop ads that resonate with your target audience, utilizing compelling visuals and copy. Continuously test and optimize your ads for better performance.

PROS AND CONS OF PPC MARKETING
PROS

- **Immediate traffic.** Unlike organic methods, PPC can drive immediate traffic to your website.

- **Targeted reach.** PPC platforms offer sophisticated targeting options, allowing you to reach specific demographics, interests, and behaviors.

- **Measurable results.** Every aspect of PPC campaigns is measurable, from the cost per click to the conversion rate, enabling you to understand the effectiveness of your ads.

CONS

- **Costs can escalate.** Without proper management, PPC can become expensive, especially in competitive industries.
- **Requires expertise.** Effective PPC campaigns require an understanding of ad platforms, targeting, and optimization strategies.
- **Short-lived impact.** PPC drives traffic only as long as you pay for clicks. Unlike organic strategies, traffic ceases once the campaign ends.

ACTION STEPS FOR SUCCESSFUL PPC CAMPAIGNS

1. **Create and launch your ad.** Start by crafting an ad that aligns with your brand message and appeals to your target audience. Launch it on one of the Big Three platforms.
2. **Monitor and manage costs.** Keep a close watch on your spending. Set a budget and adjust bids to ensure you're not overspending for clicks.
3. **Optimize for conversion.** Continuously analyze the performance of your ads. Test different

elements like headlines, images, and calls to action to improve click-through rates and conversions.

4. **Scale wisely.** Once you find a winning formula, gradually scale your ads. Avoid rapid scaling, as it can lead to unmanageable costs and diminishing returns.

SCALING YOUR PPC EFFORTS

1. **Gradually increase your budget.** As your ads start to perform well, incrementally increase your budget to boost visibility without risking a significant financial hit.

2. **Expand your targeting.** Explore broader or different audience segments to increase reach while maintaining ad relevance.

3. **Refine and repeat.** Use the data from your campaigns to refine your strategy. Replicate successful tactics and discard underperforming elements.

PPC advertising requires a strategic approach, balancing costs with potential returns. While it can be a powerful tool for quick visibility and targeted reach, it also demands ongoing management and careful optimization to maximize its effectiveness.

Phase 4: Speaking

Speaking is a very powerful avenue for attracting clients and scaling your business, because it allows for direct engagement with your audience and immediately establishes you as an authority in your field. Here's a detailed examination of speaking as a client attraction strategy.

TYPES OF SPEAKING ENGAGEMENTS

1. **Speak to sell.** These are events where you directly pitch your products or services at the end of your talk. It's crucial to balance valuable content with your sales pitch to maintain credibility.

2. **Speak to collect leads.** Here, the goal is to gather leads rather than make immediate sales. Offer a free resource in exchange for contact information, building your email list for future marketing.

3. **Consulting.** Offering your expertise in a consulting capacity can be lucrative. It involves deeper engagement with clients on specific challenges or projects.

4. **Your own events (virtual or live).** Hosting your own live or virtual events gives you complete

control over the content and the sales process. This can include workshops, webinars, online challenges, and/or conferences.

ACTION STEPS TO BOOK SPEAKING ENGAGEMENTS

1. **Event selection.** Identify events that align with your expertise and target audience. Consider the event's reach, audience demographics, and the potential for lead generation or sales.

2. **Connect with meeting planners.** Research and reach out to event planners. Tailor your pitch to show how your talk adds value to their event.

3. **Pitching.** Develop a compelling pitch that highlights your unique perspective, expertise, and the benefits your talk offers to the audience.

4. **Delivering value.** Ensure your talk provides actionable insights and real value. This builds trust and positions you as an authority.

5. **Continuing the transformation.** Offer ways for the audience to engage further, such as through a free resource, a product, or a consultation.

PROS AND CONS OF SPEAKING TO ATTRACT CLIENTS
PROS

- **Direct engagement.** Speaking allows for personal interaction, creating a stronger connection with potential clients.

- **Authority building.** Regular speaking engagements establish you as an expert in your field.
- **Lead generation.** Speaking events are excellent for collecting high-quality leads.

CONS

- **Preparation time.** Crafting and practicing your talk requires significant time and effort.
- **Finding opportunities.** Securing speaking engagements can be competitive and time-consuming.
- **Travel and logistics.** In-person events involve travel, which can be costly and time-intensive.

SCALING YOUR SPEAKING ENGAGEMENTS

- **Build a speaker profile.** Create a compelling speaker profile highlighting your expertise, past talks, and testimonials.
- **Network.** Attend industry events to network with other professionals and event organizers.
- **Leverage social media.** Use platforms like LinkedIn to showcase your speaking engagements and connect with potential clients.
- **Record your talks.** Use recordings to promote your speaking skills and reach a broader audience online.

By strategically leveraging speaking engagements, you can significantly enhance your visibility, establish authority, and attract high-quality clients to scale your business effectively.

Example: To see examples of my past speaking engagements and book me to speak at your next conference or event, visit **BookNoah.com**.

Phase 5: Search Engine Optimization

Search engine optimization (SEO) is a crucial strategy for attracting clients by enhancing the visibility of your website in search engines' organic results. Here's a detailed look at SEO as a client attraction method.

UNDERSTANDING SEO

SEO involves optimizing your website and content to appear higher in search engine results pages (SERPs). This is achieved by focusing on key elements such as keywords, content quality, site structure, and backlinks.

ACTION STEPS FOR SEO

1. **Content creation.** Develop blog posts or videos centered around topics relevant to your target market. Use keywords effectively to improve search rankings.

2. **Ranking in search engines.** SEO tactics aim to rank your content higher on search engines like Google, making it more visible to potential clients.

3. **Attracting prospects via search.** Potential clients find your content through search engines, which can lead them to your website.

4. **Converting visitors to clients.** Engaging, high-quality content can persuade visitors to explore your products or services and ultimately make a purchase.

PROS AND CONS OF SEO
PROS

- **Cost-effective.** Once ranked, SEO brings in organic traffic without the ongoing costs associated with paid advertising.
- **Long-term results.** Effective SEO can provide sustained traffic over time.
- **Credibility and trust.** High search engine rankings can enhance the perceived credibility of your business.

CONS

- **Time-consuming.** SEO results are not immediate. It can take months to see significant improvement in rankings.

- **Constantly evolving.** Search engines frequently update their algorithms, requiring ongoing adaptation of your SEO strategies.
- **Technical complexity.** Effective SEO involves various technical aspects, including site structure, mobile optimization, and more.

COMMON PITFALLS OF SEO

- **Keyword stuffing.** Overusing keywords can lead to penalties from search engines.
- **Neglecting mobile optimization.** With the increase in mobile searches, having a mobile-friendly site is crucial.
- **Ignoring user experience.** SEO isn't just about pleasing search engines; user experience plays a significant role in rankings.

SCALING UP SEO

- **Regular content updates.** Continuously add fresh, relevant content to your site to maintain and improve your search rankings.
- **Backlink strategy.** Develop a strategy to acquire high-quality backlinks from reputable websites.
- **Analytics and monitoring.** Use tools like Google Analytics to monitor your site's performance and make data-driven decisions.
- **SEO audits.** Regularly audit your site for

SEO performance and make necessary improvements.

- **Local SEO.** If your business serves a local market, optimize for local search terms and listings.

SEO is a powerful tool for client attraction, offering long-term, cost-effective results. It requires a strategic approach, consistent effort, and adaptation to search engine updates. However, when done correctly, SEO not only improves your site's visibility but also enhances user experience, ultimately helping to convert visitors into clients.

Example: To see examples of my blogs and videos used for SEO, visit **NoahStJohn.com/blog**.

Phase 6: Social Media Marketing

Social media marketing (SMM) is the strategic use of social media platforms to promote and market your products or services. It's a vital component of modern digital marketing strategies.

ACTION STEPS FOR SMM

1. **Create social media profiles.** Establish a presence on major platforms like YouTube, Facebook, LinkedIn, Instagram, and Pinterest.

Each platform serves different content preferences and demographics.

2. **Use brand management platforms.** Sign up for Hootsuite or similar social media management tools to streamline posting across platforms.

3. **Brand consistency.** Ensure all your social media profiles reflect your brand identity for recognition and consistency.

4. **Regular posting.** Maintain an active presence by posting engaging and shareable content 3 to 5 times daily on each platform.

PROS AND CONS OF SMM
PROS

- **Wide reach.** Social media platforms have massive user bases, providing access to a large audience.

- **Engagement.** Allows for direct interaction with your audience, building relationships and loyalty.

- **Brand awareness.** Regular posting helps in building brand recognition and visibility.

- **Cost-effectiveness.** Many aspects of social media marketing are free or relatively low-cost compared to traditional marketing channels.

CONS

- **Time-consuming.** Maintaining an active social media presence requires significant time and effort.
- **Algorithm changes.** Social platforms frequently change their algorithms, impacting visibility and engagement.
- **Potential for negative feedback.** Open platforms mean anyone can post negative comments or feedback, which needs to be managed effectively.

WHAT TO WATCH OUT FOR

- **Inconsistent branding.** Ensure all your social media profiles are uniformly branded.
- **Overpromotion.** Too much promotion can deter followers. Balance promotional content with informative and engaging posts.
- **Ignoring engagement.** Failing to engage with your audience can harm your brand's reputation and miss opportunities for relationship building.

SCALING UP SMM

- **Content calendar.** Develop a content calendar to plan and schedule posts in advance.

- **Analytics tools.** Use analytics tools provided by social platforms to track engagement and refine your strategy.
- **Paid advertising.** Utilize paid social media advertising to boost reach and target specific demographics.
- **Influencer partnerships.** Collaborate with influencers to expand your reach and credibility.
- **Cross-promotion.** Leverage your presence on one platform to grow your audience on another.
- **Community building.** Foster a community around your brand by encouraging discussions and interactions.

Social media marketing is a dynamic and essential tool for attracting clients. When you balance your promotional content with engagement and value, you can significantly enhance your visibility, build your brand, and attract clients for little or no cost.

Examples: Follow me on all my social media channels:

- **WatchNoahTV.com (YouTube channel)**
- **Facebook.com/noahstjohn**
- **Instagram.com/noahstjohn**
- **Tiktok.com/noahstjohn.com**
- **Linkedin.com/in/noahstjohn**

Elena's Story

Elena, a passionate health and wellness coach, had been struggling to gain traction in her online business. Despite her expertise and dedication, her client base remained limited. That was until she joined my 12-Week Breakthrough coaching program and began implementing my MAPSSS Method.

Elena enrolled in the program with high hopes, but little idea of how transformative the experience would be. In short order, my MAPSSS Method became her roadmap to success.

Elena began by targeting health and wellness podcasts and local radio shows. With a well-crafted pitch, she secured guest appearances, sharing her insights and connecting with a broader audience.

Leveraging her new-found confidence, Elena started speaking at health and wellness seminars and workshops. These engagements positioned her as an authority in her field.

Elena also revamped her website and blog with SEO-friendly content, steadily climbing the ranks in search engine results, attracting organic traffic. She then strengthened her presence on platforms like Instagram and LinkedIn, sharing valuable content and engaging with her growing community.

Elena's business experienced a remarkable transformation. Her client base grew, not just in numbers but in engagement and loyalty. She began receiving inquiries from people who discovered her through various MAPSSS channels, each resonating with different aspects of her outreach.

Elena's journey is an example of how the right strategies, coupled with determination and guidance, can transform a struggling online business into a successful, influential brand.

The Importance of Taking Action Now

My MAPSSS Method for Client Attraction is a potent and comprehensive approach to building and scaling your online business. It encompasses a variety of strategies, each crucial for reaching your ideal clients and establishing a sustainable, profitable online presence.

I know that it's easy to feel overwhelmed by the sheer breadth of these strategies, but the key to success is to start small and build gradually. Start with the phase you're most comfortable with or which seems most accessible. Define achievable objectives for each phase and work steadily towards them.

Most successful online entrepreneurs started with little or nothing. While the journey might seem daunting, with each step you'll gain confidence and momentum. My MAPSSS Method isn't just a strategy; it's a roadmap to turning your vision into reality. Start today, and you'll be amazed at what you can achieve!

IF YOU DELAY THE START, YOU'LL PLAY A LESSER PART.

In our next chapter, I'll reveal my 7-Figure Scaling Secrets so you can boost your income and amplify your impact faster and easier. Are you ready to scale up and soar?

6

My 7-Figure Scaling Secrets

It's not the best person or the best product who wins; it's the one who's best at communicating their message and their value to the world.

—NOAH ST. JOHN

In business, scaling from 6 to 7 figures and beyond is part science, part art form, demanding a synergistic blend of strategy, insight, and persistence. While the journey is unique for each entrepreneur, there are universal principles that guide successful business growth. At the heart of these principles lie the three fundamental ways to grow your business:

acquiring more customers, increasing customer spending, and *optimizing buying frequency.*

Acquiring More Customers: The Art of Expansion

The first step towards scaling your business is expanding your customer base. This is about reaching new markets, tapping into unexplored demographics, and making your products or services known to a wider audience.

The goal here is *acquisition*, a crucial phase that demands a deep understanding of your target market, a robust marketing strategy, and a relentless pursuit of growth opportunities. Whether it's through innovative marketing campaigns, strategic partnerships, or leveraging digital platforms, acquiring more customers lays the foundation for your business's expansion.

Increasing Customer Spending: The Art of Maximizing Value

Growth isn't just about numbers; it's also about value. The second pillar of scaling your business involves encouraging your existing customers to spend more. This strategy, known as *monetization*, focuses on maximizing the value of each customer interaction.

It can be achieved through upselling, cross-selling, or offering premium services or products. The key here is to deeply understand your customers' needs and desires, providing them with irresistible offers that enhance their experience and increase their spending.

Enhancing Buying Frequency: The Art of Cultivating Loyalty

The third strategy is all about *optimization*: increasing the frequency with which your customers buy from you. This involves turning one-time buyers into repeat customers and creating a loyal customer base that consistently chooses your products or services.

By providing exceptional customer service, maintaining high product quality, and implementing loyalty programs or incentives, you can create a business environment that draws customers back as well as turning them into advocates for your brand.

As we explore each of these strategies in this chapter, remember that scaling a business is a dynamic process. It requires a careful balance of these three elements, tailored to the unique contours of your business and market. Let's explore how to master these three fundamental ways to grow your business, paving your path to seven-figure success and beyond.

Phase 1: Get More Customers: Acquisition Strategies

Expanding your customer base is a pivotal step in scaling your business. Below is a breakdown of the top 17 "free" ways to acquire customers.

(I put the word "free" in quotation marks because while you don't necessarily have to pay for any of these strategies, nothing is actually free. In other words, you'll have to spend time, energy, and focus in order to make any or all of these methods work. However, I have used every single one of these strategies to grow my business, and each of them can be highly effective for driving traffic and increasing sales.)

1. **Book or ebook.** Publishing a book or ebook is a powerful way to establish authority in your field. It can serve as a detailed business card, providing valuable insights while directing readers to your other services or products.

2. **Samples and trials.** Offering free samples or trial periods of your product or service allows potential customers to experience the value firsthand, increasing the likelihood of conversion.

3. **Quizzes and surveys.** Interactive tools like quizzes or surveys engage potential customers, offering personalized insights or

recommendations based on their responses, which can be a gateway to your offerings.

4. **Free consultation or strategy session.** Providing a free consultation or strategy session positions you as a trusted advisor and showcases the potential value of your full services.

5. **Podcast.** Hosting or guesting on podcasts can reach a vast audience. The podcast is a platform to share expertise, stories, and subtly promote your offerings.

6. **Your own blog.** A blog drives traffic to your website through SEO, establishes your expertise, and keeps your audience engaged with valuable content.

7. **Webinars.** Hosting webinars on topics relevant to your target market can attract potential customers by offering them valuable insights and a taste of your expertise.

8. **Virtual events.** Participating in or hosting virtual events exposes your brand to a larger audience and establishes connections in your industry.

9. **Channel selling.** Utilizing platforms like Amazon or eBay can put your products in front of a vast audience that's already looking to purchase.

10. **Facebook organic marketing (non-PPC).** Leveraging Facebook through organic methods

like pages, groups, and events can build community and engagement around your brand.

11. **LinkedIn organic (posts and groups).** LinkedIn is ideal for B2B networking. Regular posts and active group participation can establish you as a thought leader.

12. **YouTube organic.** A YouTube channel with compelling content can significantly increase your visibility and position you as an expert in your field.

13. **Instagram.** Utilizing Instagram's visual platform for brand storytelling and engagement can attract a dedicated following.

14. **Search engine optimization (SEO).** Optimizing your website content for search engines like Google, Yahoo, and Bing increases your visibility to those searching for related topics or products.

15. **Affiliates, joint ventures, and referrals.** Collaborating with others in your industry for mutual promotion or using referral incentives can exponentially increase your reach.

16. **Public relations.** Gaining media coverage in radio, TV, print, or online can dramatically increase brand awareness and credibility.

17. **Public speaking.** Speaking at events, whether in-person or virtual, can position you as an authority and open doors to new customer relationships.

Each of these strategies offers unique advantages and can be used in combination to create a robust customer acquisition plan. By implementing these methods, you can significantly enhance your business's visibility and appeal to a broader audience, laying the groundwork for sustainable growth and success.

Top 10 Paid Methods to Acquire Customers

Investing in paid strategies can accelerate your customer acquisition. Here's a detailed breakdown of the top 10 paid methods to acquire customers.

1. **Online catalog** (your own ecommerce site). Creating an online catalog on your ecommerce site allows for a centralized showcase of your products or services. It's a direct way to facilitate purchases.

2. **Facebook paid advertising.** Utilizing Facebook's paid advertising features can target specific demographics and interests, making your ads more effective and reaching a broader audience.

3. **Instagram paid ads.** Paid promotions on Instagram can significantly increase your reach, especially among a younger and visually oriented demographic.

4. **LinkedIn paid ads.** LinkedIn's paid advertising is ideal for B2B marketing, allowing you to

target professionals and decision-makers in specific industries.

5. **YouTube paid ads.** Investing in YouTube ads can capture the attention of a vast audience and is particularly effective for visual and engaging content.

6. **Google AdWords** (search network). This approach targets users actively searching for keywords related to your business, offering high intent to purchase or engage.

7. **Google AdWords** (display network). These ads appear on various websites across the Internet, enhancing brand visibility and recall.

8. **Email advertising.** Paying for placements in popular newsletters or promotional emails can reach a targeted audience already interested in related topics.

9. **Bing/Yahoo PPC.** Although they have a smaller market share than Google, advertising on these platforms can be less competitive and more cost-effective.

10. **Direct mail.** Sending physical mail to potential customers can stand out in an increasingly digital world and can be especially effective for local businesses or specific demographics.

Free versus Paid Customer Acquisition: Pros and Cons

FREE CUSTOMER ACQUISITION

Pros. Cost-effective, builds organic relationships, enhances credibility, often leads to more loyal customers.

Cons. Time-consuming, requires consistent effort, slower to scale, unpredictable results.

PAID CUSTOMER ACQUISITION

Pros. Faster results, scalable, more control over targeting and reach, measurable ROI.

Cons. Can be expensive, requires ongoing investment, risk of ad fatigue, less personal connection with the audience.

Free methods are ideal for building long-term, organic growth and establishing credibility. Paid methods, on the other hand, offer quick, scalable results and precise targeting.

The best approach often involves a mix of both, leveraging the strengths of each to create a comprehensive customer acquisition strategy. This blended approach maximizes reach and efficiency, ensuring a steady flow of new customers while nurturing a loyal base.

Phase 2: Get Them to Spend More: Monetization Strategies

Encouraging customers to spend more is crucial for maximizing revenue. Here's a breakdown of the top 7 activation strategies for monetization:

1. Immediate Upsells

What it is: Offering an additional, related product or service immediately after a customer makes a purchase.

Why it's important: Increases average order value and capitalizes on the buyer's readiness to spend.

Example: Selling an extended warranty or premium version at checkout.

2. High-Ticket Upsells

What it is: Upselling more expensive, premium products or services.

Why it matters: Targets customers willing to pay more for enhanced features or services.

Example: Upgrading a basic service package to a comprehensive one.

3. Bundles and Kits

What it is: Combining multiple products or services into a single package.

Why it matters: Encourages purchasing more items while offering more value and convenience.

Example: A skin care bundle with cleanser, toner, and moisturizer.

4. Subscription and Membership Programs

What it is: Offering products or services on a recurring basis.

Why it matters: Ensures a steady revenue stream while building customer loyalty.

Example: Monthly subscription boxes or access to exclusive content.

5. Corporate Consulting and Training

What it is: Providing specialized services to businesses.

Why it matters: Accesses a market willing to pay higher rates for specialized expertise.

Example: Customized training programs for employees.

6. Downsells and Cross-sells

What it is: Offering lower-priced alternatives (downsells) or additional products (cross-sells).

Why it matters: Maximizes revenue per customer; caters to varied needs and budgets.

Example: Suggesting a smaller package as a downsell or a complementary product as a cross-sell.

7. Done for You Services

What it is: Offering complete, ready-to-use solutions.

Why it matters: Appeals to customers looking for convenience and expertise.

Example: Managing a client's social media accounts.

These strategies, when executed correctly, not only boost revenue but also deepen the customer relationship by providing more value. Each approach caters to different customer needs and preferences, allowing for a diverse range of monetization opportunities.

By strategically implementing these methods, you can significantly enhance your profitability without necessarily increasing your customer base, which will lead to increased profits and even happier customers.

Phase 3: Increase Buying Frequency: Optimization Strategies

Many business owners focus most of their time, money, and energy on acquiring new customers. While this isn't wrong, it's not the most efficient or effective way to scale your business.

Did you know that acquiring a new customer can cost 5 to 10 times more than retaining an existing one? Moreover, a retained long-term customer tends to spend more than a newly acquired customer. As much as 80 percent of a company's revenue can come from 20 percent of its existing customer base, and improving your customer retention by just 5 percent can increase profits from 25 to 95 percent.

These numbers underscore the importance of focusing on your existing customers, as it's not only more cost-effective but also significantly boosts your profits. It highlights why businesses should prioritize customer retention strategies alongside acquisition tactics in their growth and scaling efforts.

Because this is such a critical step in scaling your business, I'm listing the top 8 customer optimization strategies below. By implementing them, you can create a loyal customer base that not only buys more often, but also spends more per transaction. This multipronged approach ensures a sustained and growing revenue stream, which is vital for the long-term success and scaling of your business.

1. Regular Email Newsletter

What it is: Sending consistent email updates, tips, or news to subscribers.

Why it matters: Keeps your brand top-of-mind; builds a routine communication channel.

Example: A weekly newsletter sharing industry insights, new product announcements, and special offers.

2. Automated Email Follow-up

What it is: A series of automated emails triggered by specific customer actions.

Why it matters: Personalizes the customer experience; maintains engagement after purchase.

Example: A welcome email series for new subscribers, or postpurchase follow-up emails.

3. Exit Offers

What it is: Special offers presented to users attempting to leave your website.

Why it matters: Captures potentially lost sales and incentivizes customers to reconsider their decision.

Example: A pop-up offering a discount or free shipping if a customer tries to exit the checkout page.

4. Retargeting on Social Media and High-Traffic Blogs

What it is: Displaying ads to users who have previously visited your website.

Why it matters: Reminds past visitors of your products and services and encourages repeat visits.

Example: Facebook ads targeting users who visited your product pages but didn't make a purchase.

5. SMS Marketing

What it is: Short message servicing (SMS) is sending marketing messages via text messages.

Why it matters: Direct and immediate communication channel; high open rates.

Example: Text message alerts about exclusive deals or new product launches.

6. Direct Mail to Existing Customer Base

What it is: Mailing physical promotional materials to current customers.

Why it matters: Offers a tangible touchpoint; can feel more personal than digital communication.

Example: Sending a catalog or a special offer postcard to existing customers.

7. Outbound Phone Follow-up

What it is: Making phone calls to existing customers for feedback or offering new products.

Why it matters: Direct, personal engagement along with the opportunity for immediate upsell or feedback.

Example: Calling customers after purchase to ensure satisfaction and introduce additional services.

8. Customer Appreciation Sales and Offers

What it is: Special promotions or discounts exclusively for existing customers.

Why it matters: Rewards loyalty and encourages repeat purchases.

Example: Offering a customers-only discount during the holiday season or on customer anniversaries.

Bill's Story

Bill is a small business owner in the digital marketing space with a vision to scale his business, but who felt stuck in a loop of moderate success. Despite his efforts, he struggled to move beyond a certain revenue threshold. That's when he discovered my 12-Week Breakthrough coaching program and decided to take a leap of faith.

Bill began by focusing on acquiring more customers. He tapped into the power of organic Facebook marketing, leveraging his existing network to spread word-of-mouth about his services. By consistently providing valuable content and engaging with his audience, Bill saw a steady increase in his customer base.

With a growing customer base, Bill shifted his focus to increasing the value of each customer. He introduced a range of upsell options, including premium services and exclusive content, tailored to his diverse clientele.

He also launched a subscription model for his digital marketing tools, offering a steady and predictable revenue stream. Bill quickly noticed that his existing clients were more than willing to invest in these additional offerings, significantly increasing his average revenue per customer.

Within just 12 weeks, Bill's business transformed. His customer base doubled, the average spend per customer increased by 50 percent, and his clients began purchasing more frequently. He credits the 12-Week Breakthrough coaching program for providing him with the strategies he needed and instilling the confidence to execute them effectively.

If You Wait Too Long, The Opportunity's Gone

The digital age has accelerated market changes, making agility and prompt decision-making more critical than ever. In scaling your 7-Figure Machine, understanding the fast-moving nature of opportunities is key.

Every market shift, technological advancement, or trend creates a window of opportunity. Being the first or early in exploiting these changes can set you apart from competitors. However, these windows don't stay open forever. Delaying action means risking the closure of these lucrative openings, leaving you to face the tougher climb of catching up or breaking into saturated spaces.

Procrastination or indecision is often rooted in the fear of making imperfect choices. In business, the cost of inaction usually outweighs the risks of imperfect action. While you wait for the "perfect moment" or "more information," the opportunity can slip away, and with it the potential exponential growth for your business.

Although I'm emphasizing speed, I'm not advocating recklessness. The phrase "money loves speed" means taking calculated yet swift actions based on the best available information and intuition honed from experience. It involves creating streamlined decision-making processes, staying informed about market trends, and having the courage to leap when opportunities present themselves.

I'M ENCOURAGING ACTION, NOT RECKLESSNESS.

The world of business rewards those who can ride the wave of change, not those waiting on the shore for the perfect wave. Perhaps the most significant cost of waiting too long is the realization of lost potential. It's not just about the missed financial gain but also about the growth, learning, and connections that accompany seizing opportunities.

This highlights a fundamental truth: in the journey of scaling your 7-Figure Machine, remember that time is an irreplaceable currency, and the best time to act is now. That's why I encourage you to take the next logical step if you want to go further and faster than you ever thought possible!

7

For Those Who Want to Go Further and Faster

*Lots of people have dreams and get
knocked down and don't have things go their way.
Just keep getting up and getting up, and
then you will get your breakthrough!*

—TOM BRADY

Now that this book is almost over, you have three options:

Option 1. Forget everything you just read and let this become more "shelf-help" (not recommended).

Option 2. Try to figure all this out on your own. Granted, it will take a lot more time and you might make a lot of costly mistakes, but you can do it on your own if you wish.

Option 3. Do it with me, so we can accelerate your results up to 10 times faster, with far less stress and without wasting time or effort.

So if you want to . . .

- Live the life of your dreams without stressing over finances;
- Take more vacations while making money in your sleep;
- Maximize your income without adding more hours to your workweek;
- Be dead solid perfect with your offers. Every. Single. Time;
- Have more impact, more influence and more financial freedom without having to figure it out on your own;
- . . . you're invited to join The 12-Week Breakthrough.

In just 12 short weeks, I'll give you my copy-and-paste, plug-and-play, paint-by-numbers, fill-in-the-blank templates, checklists, resources, and strategies that have generated over $33 million in online sales and more than $3.2 *billion* in found revenues for me and my clients since 1997.

Here's What This Means for You

- You don't have to go through the pain, torment and agony that I did to figure all this out on my own.
- You have hidden equity in your business right now. However . . .
- The longer you wait to get all of this in place working for you, the more money, opportunity, and wealth will slip through your fingers.

Because the more you delay, the more you'll pay.

Picture Your Life 12 Weeks from Today

Walk with me for a moment, 12 weeks from today. Imagine that we start working together right now. Did you notice how much *happier* you are now?

How you're *sleeping* better and more peacefully?

How you start the day with a sense of *joy and purpose?*

How life feels *fresh, full of potential, less constrained?*

All as a result of taking action!

As you're reading this, some more head trash may have come up. So let's address that right here and now.

HEAD TRASH: *"I'm not sure if this is a good fit for me."*

Here's what my client Adam S. has to say:

I'm here to tell you that Noah St. John's coaching is fantastic! *Since we started working with Noah, my company grew six times in size.* When you work with Noah, he focuses on removing all the things that are holding you back, whereas a lot of other people out there are all focused on pushing you forward, not realizing that when your foot is on the brake at the same time that it's on the gas pedal, you're just getting in your own way. So my recommendation, my GUARANTEE is: give coaching with Noah a shot, you're going to be 100 percent happy with it!

HEAD TRASH: *"I don't think I can afford it."*

Here's what my client Thomesa L. has to say:

Before Noah, I was a seminar junkie. Yes, I went through program after program just doing what I could to better myself personally and professionally. When I discovered Noah St. John, I had that fear of, "Is this just another program that I may get a few nuggets from and then just go back to my default program?" Well, my fear is gone! I bit the bullet, I jumped into Noah's program and I couldn't be happier, because he is DIFFERENT. *In the first two weeks, I TRIPLED my investment!* Does that make you a little more excited about where you're going to go with Noah? So I just want to say that if you are on the fence about any program that Noah is offering, GET OFF! Take action. It works. It's simple, it's practical. And you'll be amazed at what you gain from it. Thank you, Noah, for all you have taught me!

HEAD TRASH: *"What if I don't get a return on my investment?"*

Here's what my client Cledra M. has to say:

Noah's coaching created MOMENTUM in ALL areas of my life—business, health, love and more. *I made my investment back in less than 48 hours after joining!* The modules, the bonuses, the access to a community of people around the world—it's all been priceless!"

Here's What to Do Now

If you know you want this and you know you want it now, go to **12WeekBreakthrough.com/speed-now** and submit your deposit to join *The 12-Week Breakthrough.*

For instance, if you're ready right now (like my client Charles, who gave me $1 and I gave him $18 back), you can secure your spot with a small deposit. Someone from my team will contact you to make sure you're a good fit for the program.

Plus, when you submit your deposit, you'll also be eligible for a Bonus VIP Coaching Session with me!

If you want to talk with someone about the program first, go to **BreakthroughwithNoah.com** and submit your application.

As we come to the end of this book, remember the words I shared with you earlier in this book:

Napoleon Hill said, "Those who reach decisions promptly and definitely know what they want and generally get it. The leaders in every walk of life decide quickly and firmly."

W. Clement Stone said, "The greatest enemy of wealth isn't a mindset issue. It isn't access to resources. It isn't even upbringing or circumstances. The greatest enemy of wealth is delay."

Dr. Noah says, "Procrastination is the assassination of your destination."

One Final Guarantee

Ben Franklin said many years ago that there are only two guarantees in life: death and taxes. With all due respect to ol' Ben, I would argue there is, in fact, a third guarantee: *if you keep doing the same thing you're doing now, I guarantee you'll keep getting the same results you're getting now.*

Therefore, if you'd like to get BETTER results in your life and your business, I encourage you take ACTION now—because time waits for no one!

Noah St. John's coaching starts where Think and Grow Rich *and* The Secret *left off.*
—Mike Filsaime, 8-Figure CEO of Groove.cm

My company went from being stuck at $4M in sales to over $20M in sales as a result of coaching with Noah.
—Adam S., 8-figure CEO

My income is up 800 percent since I started coaching with Noah!
—Steven B., Entrepreneur

Coaching with Noah enabled me to double my business in less than twelve months after I'd been stuck at the same level for fifteen years.
—Aubrey R., Entrepreneur

In the first two weeks of coaching with Noah, I TRIPLED my investment!
—THOMESA L., ENTREPRENEUR

As a result of coaching with Noah, I doubled my income, then doubled it AGAIN in just 12 short weeks.
—Mike C., Entrepreneur

Recommended Resources

YOUR FREE BONUS GIFT

As a thank-you for purchasing this book, I would like to give you exclusive, insider access to the exact system my clients are using to instantly shatter their limiting beliefs that were putting a ceiling on their business revenue, once and for all, using ONE simple process that can take as little as 5 minutes a day.

Best of all, it works especially well even when all the other programs, seminars, methods, systems and gurus have let you down or you don't actually know what the specific problem is.

This is also the fastest and easiest way to gain special access to the lucrative system that's added more than $3.2 billion in revenue for me and my clients since 1997.

So if you . . .

- Want a proven system to instantly shatter limiting beliefs and recapture lost revenues;
- Have a business that's beyond startup phase and is actually making sales;
- Are ready for "hockey stick growth" in your company;
- Want insider access to my fill-in-the-blank templates, checklists, and resources;
- Want to know how this guaranteed system can work for you

. . . schedule your complimentary **7-Figure Breakthrough Consultation** now. We will review your business, see how this system can work for you, offer you some advice on how to use it, and (if we know we can help you) discuss how we can assist you in implementing it—GUARANTEED.

Book your 7-Figure
Breakthrough Session now at
BreakthroughwithNoah.com

Book Noah to Speak

"Noah is definitely NOT your typical motivational
speaker! I took six pages of notes during his
keynote presentation. SIMPLY PHENOMENAL—
A MUST-HAVE RESOURCE for every
organization that wants to grow!"
—Mary Kay Cosmetics

"All I heard was great feedback! Thank you, Noah, for really engaging our audience. I am recommending you as a speaker for more meetings."
—Meeting Planners International

"I highly recommend Noah St. John as a keynote speaker because he resonates on a deep emotional level with his audience. Dynamic, impactful, inspiring, motivating, and professional— in short, the PERFECT speaker!"
—City Summit & Gala

Book Noah as your keynote speaker, and you're guaranteed to make your event highly enjoyable and unforgettable.

For more than two decades, Noah St. John has consistently rated as the #1 keynote speaker by meeting planners and attendees.

His unique style combines inspiring audiences with his remarkable TRUE story, keeping them laughing with his high-energy, down-to-earth style, and empowering them with actionable strategies to take their RESULTS to the NEXT LEVEL.

Book Noah for your event at
BookNoah.com

Also Available from
Dr. Noah St. John

BREAKTHROUGH WITH NOAH

How I Help My Clients Make More in Just 12 Weeks
Than They Made in the Past 12 Months—
While Gaining 1–3 Hours per Day
and 4–8 Weeks a Year.
BreakthroughwithNoah.com

THE 7-FIGURE MACHINE

Scale Up Your Online Business Up to 10X Faster
Without the Stress, Hustle or Information Overload
7FigureMachine.com

Motivate and Inspire Others!

"SHARE THIS BOOK"

RETAIL $19.95

Special Quantity Discounts Available

To Place an Order, Contact:

(330) 871-4331

info@SuccessClinic.com

Acknowledgments

My most grateful thanks to . . .

God, the answer to all of our questions.

My beautiful wife, Babette, for being my best friend and the best Loving Mirror I've ever had. Thank you for believing in me and supporting me and for your tireless commitment to helping me put a dent in the universe.

My parents, who sacrificed and gave more than they had.

Jack Canfield, for grokking my message when it was a bunch of pages bound with a piece of tape.

Dr. Stephen R. Covey, who inspired me to get into the business of helping people when the audiocassette album of his book *The 7 Habits of Highly Effective*

People fell off a church bookshelf and landed at my feet. (I swear I'm not making that up.)

Through the years, many have shared ideas, inspiration, mentoring, and support that have impacted my life, each in a different way. While it's impossible to thank everyone, please know that I appreciate you greatly:

Alex Mandossian, Arianna Huffington, Donny Osmond, Gary Vaynerchuk, Jenny McCarthy, Joel Osteen, John Lee Dumas, Marie Forleo, Suze Orman, Ashley Grayson, Bill and Steve Harrison, Dan Bova, Dr. Fabrizio Mancini, Grant Cardone, Harvey Mackay, Jason Hewlett, Jay Abraham, Jeff Lerner, Jeff Magee, Jeffrey Hayzlett, Jen Groover, Joe Vitale, John Assaraf, John Cito, Dr. John Gray, Jon Benson, Mike Filsaime, Nathan Osmond, Neale Donald Walsch, Peter Hoppenfeld, Rich Schefren, Richard Rossi, Russell Brunson, Tom Junod, Verne Harnish, and so many other people who have inspired me in my career!

Very special thanks to the vast and growing tribe of our phenomenal coaching clients around the world who believe in the power of this message. Thank you for spreading the word about my work to all corners of the globe!

Every day, as I hear more and more stories of how the coaching work we do together is changing lives, you inspire, encourage, and uplift me.

I am humbled by your stories of how my work has changed your lives—truly, more than you know. Whether you're a member of our Coaching Family, attend one of our virtual events or online trainings this year, or simply commit to telling your friends about this book, I'm grateful for you.

Every day brings with it the opportunity to be reborn in the next greatest version of ourselves.

NOW IT'S YOUR TURN

I LOOK FORWARD TO BEING A PART OF *YOUR* SUCCESS STORY!

About the Author

Noah St. John, PhD, is recognized as "The Father of AFFORMATIONS®" and "The Mental Health Coach to the Stars."

Working with Hollywood celebrities, 7- and 8-figure company CEOs, professional athletes, top executives, and elite entrepreneurs, Noah is famous for helping his coaching clients make more in just 12 weeks than they did in the previous 12 months, while gaining 1–3 hours per day and 4–8 weeks a year.

Noah's clients are the 0.1 percent rock stars who love to *take action* and get amazing *results!*

Noah is also the only author in history to have works published by HarperCollins, Hay House,

Simon & Schuster, Mindvalley, Nightingale-Conant, and the publisher of the Chicken Soup for the Soul series. His twenty-five books have been published in 19 languages worldwide.

Noah's mission is to eliminate not-enoughness from the world. He is internationally known for his signature coaching services and facilitating workshops at companies and institutions across the globe. Noah delivers private workshops, virtual events, and online courses, which his audiences call "*mandatory* for anyone who wants to succeed in life and business."

One of the most requested, in-demand business and motivational keynote speakers in the world, Noah is famous for having the Midas touch, because his clients have added more than $3.2 billion in found revenues. His sought-after advice is known as the "secret sauce" to business and personal growth.

He also appears frequently in the news worldwide, including ABC, NBC, CBS, FOX, The Hallmark Channel, National Public Radio, *Chicago Sun-Times*, *Parade*, *Los Angeles Business Journal*, *The Washington Post*, *Woman's Day*, *Entrepreneurs on Fire*, *Selling Power*, Entrepreneur.com, *The Jenny McCarthy Show*, *Costco Connection*, and *SUCCESS* magazine.

Fun fact: Noah once won an all-expenses-paid trip to Hawaii on the game show *Concentration*, where he missed winning a new car by three seconds. (Note: He had not yet discovered his Afformations® Method or Power Habits® Formula.)

Book Noah to speak for your next virtual or live event, conference or seminar at **BookNoah.com**.

Printed in the USA
CPSIA information can be obtained
at www.ICGtesting.com
JSHW012237070624
64474JS00003B/29